# Eggs

## Nourishing recipes
### for health and wellness

This edition published by Parragon Books Ltd in 2016
LOVE FOOD is an imprint of Parragon Books Ltd

Parragon Books Ltd
Chartist House
15–17 Trim Street
Bath BA1 1HA, UK
www.parragon.com/lovefood

ISBN: 978-1-4748-1770-7

Printed in China

Cover photography by Tony Briscoe
New recipes by Teresa Goldfinch
New recipe photography by Kris Kirkham
New home economy by Lucy-Ruth Hathaway

Notes for the Reader
This book uses both metric and imperial measurements. Follow the same units of measurement throughout; do not mix metric and imperial. All spoon measurements are level: teaspoons are assumed to be 5 ml, and tablespoons are assumed to be 15 ml. Unless otherwise stated, milk is assumed to be full fat, eggs and individual fruits and vegetables are medium, pepper is freshly ground black pepper and salt is table salt. A pinch of salt is calculated as $\frac{1}{16}$ of a teaspoon. Unless otherwise stated, all root vegetables should be peeled prior to using.

The times given are an approximate guide only. Preparation times differ according to the techniques used by different people and the cooking times may also vary from those given.

Please note that any ingredients stated as being optional are not included in the nutritional values provided. The nutritional values given are approximate and provided as a guideline only, they do not account for individual cooks, scales and portion sizes. The nutritional values provided are per serving or per item.

While the publisher of the book and the original author(s) of the recipes and other text have made all reasonable efforts to ensure that the information contained in this book is accurate and up to date at the time of publication, anyone reading this book should note the following important points: -

Medical and pharmaceutical knowledge is constantly changing and the author(s) and the publisher cannot and do not guarantee the accuracy or appropriateness of the contents of this book.

In any event, this book is not intended to be, and should not be relied upon, as a substitute for appropriate, tailored professional advice. Both the author(s) and the publisher strongly recommend that a doctor or other healthcare professional is consulted before embarking on major dietary changes.

For the reasons set out above, and to the fullest extent permitted by law, the author(s) and publisher: (i) cannot and do not accept any legal duty of care or responsibility in relation to the accuracy or appropriateness of the contents of this book, even where expressed as 'advice' or using other words to this effect; and (ii) disclaim any liability, loss, damage or risk that may be claimed or incurred as a consequence – directly or indirectly – of the use and/or application of any of the contents of this book.

For best results, use a food thermometer when cooking meat. Check the latest government guidelines for current advice.

# Contents

# Introduction

Eggs have been an important part of our diet since prehistory. Wild fowl have been domesticated in India since as early as 3200 BC, although domesticated hens have been in Europe only since 600 BC, when jungle fowl native to tropical and subtropical Southeast Asia and India were brought there. Originally quail and ostrich would have been the main source of eggs. In ancient Rome eggs were often preserved and then served as a course in their own right. It's believed that the first hens were taken to the Americas by Columbus on his second voyage there in 1493.

Of course, we now eat more hen eggs than any other type, and there are many variants available, from hens reared in different ways – including organic, free range and barn – to more varieties from different breeds of hen. It's also becoming easier to buy eggs from other species of bird, most commonly ducks, geese and quails.

# Common Varieties & Breeds

### HEN
Breeds of hens are categorized as either heavy or light. The heavy breeds (Welsummer and Marans being two of the most popular) produce darker, brown eggs, while the light breeds (such as the White Leghorn) lay white or light-coloured eggs. The normal weight range for a hen egg is somewhere between 50–75 g/1¾–2¾ oz, and they are available all year round.

### BANTAM
Bantams are small, rare-breed hens and they produce small eggs weighing 30–40 g/1–1½ oz. The ratio of yolk to white is 50:50, which is much higher than that of a standard hen egg. The intense dark yolk is perfect for scrambling or for making quiches and tarts.

### DUCK
The larger duck eggs tend to weigh 85–90 g/3–3¼ oz. Their higher fat content and light, creamy yolks make them richer than hen eggs. They are available all year round.

### GOOSE
The translucent ivory shells of these eggs are unique, as is their size. They weigh in at 180–200 g/6¼–7 oz each, making them really substantial. One goose egg is the equivalent of 2½ medium hen eggs. The flavour is rich and creamy. They are seasonal, so check availability.

### QUAIL
These tiny eggs are a quarter of the size of hen eggs and are very cute! Their small speckled shells contain delicate eggs with pale yolks. It takes just 30 seconds to soft boil them and they're perfect for canapés. They are available all year round.

### THE LESS WELL-KNOWN
As well as these common varieties, there are also those less well-known eggs that, if you can find them, will add a little wow-factor to any dinner party.

Why not seek out rhea eggs? The rhea closely resembles an ostrich and provides large eggs that are light and fluffy and highly versatile. They are seasonal, so check availability.

If you want to try an actual ostrich egg, you will need to check when they are available and just be sure you allow enough time to cook them as they can take 50 minutes simply to soft boil and a rather lengthy 2 hours to hard boil!

Another overlooked variety is that of the guinea fowl, which are small and delicate. They are seasonal, so check availability. You can also try pheasant eggs which have beautiful olive-green and brown shells and a rich flavour. Pheasant eggs are also seasonal, so check availability.

# Perfect Eggs

The benefits of eating eggs cannot be underestimated. A medium hen egg contains around 70 calories and is a good source of all the essential nutrients. Eggs contain high-quality protein, the macronutrient that best satisfies hunger. They also contain essential vitamins, including vitamin A, needed for healthy skin and good vision; vitamin D, which is deficient in many people's diets; vitamin E, which may help reduce the incidence of heart disease, certain cancers and strokes; and B vitamins. Vitamin B2 is needed for metabolizing food and vitamin B12 helps brain function and provides energy. B12 is often lacking in the diet of vegetarians and older people.

Eggs also contain essential minerals, such as phosphorous, which is essential for strong bones and teeth; iodine, which is important for thyroid function; and selenium, which is thought to protect against certain cancers. They also contain trace elements, including iron, which helps with red blood cell formation, and zinc, which supports the immune system.

The protein in eggs is extremely high quality, and is a 'complete' protein. This means that it contains all eight of the essential amino acids. Its quality is comparable to that of beef or milk and is very easily digestible.

Some eggs now contain omega-3 fatty acids, depending on what they have been fed – always check the packaging to be sure. Eggs were once criticized for their high cholesterol content but this has reduced in recent times with improvements in hen feed. It's now been shown that saturated fat in the diet has the greatest impact on blood cholesterol levels.

## EGG SAFETY

Eating raw eggs or eggs with runny yolks, or any food containing uncooked, lightly cooked or raw eggs can cause food poisoning. This is especially important for anyone in an 'at risk' group, such as:

• Babies and toddlers
• The elderly
• Pregnant women
• People who are already unwell

This is because eggs may contain salmonella bacteria, which can cause very serious illness.

People who do not belong to one of the at risk categories and eat foods containing lightly cooked eggs should not experience any health problems, but cooking eggs thoroughly is always the safest option if you are concerned about food poisoning.

# Breakfast & Snacks

HEALTHY BREAKFAST FRITTATA 13

EGG WHITE OMELETTE 14

ASPARAGUS, SALMON & POACHED EGG 17

HAM & EGG CUPS 19

POACHED EGGS & KALE WITH SOURDOUGH 20

KNOW YOUR EGGS 22

DUCK EGGS BENEDICT 25

CHIVE SCRAMBLED EGGS WITH BRIOCHE 26

POLENTA CAKES WITH POACHED EGGS 29

MUSHROOM & EGG CUPS  30

TEA-SOAKED EGGS  33

CHORIZO & QUAIL'S EGG TOASTS 34

DEVILLED EGGS 37

SPICY OVEN-BAKED SCOTCH EGGS 39

PERFECT PICKLED EGGS  40

# Healthy Breakfast Frittata

*Serve this frittata straight from the pan with home-made wholemeal bread, or wrap it in baking paper and foil and enjoy it cold at work.*

| SERVES: | PREP: *15 mins* |
|---|---|
| 4 | COOK: *20 mins* |

**PER SERVING:** *241 Kcals | 15.1g fat | 3.5g sat fat | 13.7g carbs | 2.6g sugar 2.9g fibre | 13.2g protein | 1.1g salt*

## INGREDIENTS

*250 g/9 oz baby new potatoes, unpeeled and sliced*
*2 tbsp virgin olive oil*
*4 spring onions, thinly sliced*
*1 courgette, thinly sliced*
*115 g/4 oz baby spinach, destalked*
*large pinch of smoked hot paprika*
*6 eggs*
*sea salt and pepper (optional)*

1. Bring a saucepan of water to the boil, add the potatoes and cook for 5 minutes, or until just tender, then drain well.

2. Meanwhile, heat 1 tablespoon of oil in a large ovenproof frying pan over a medium heat. Add the spring onions, courgette and potatoes and fry, stirring and turning the vegetables, for 5 minutes, or until just beginning to brown.

3. Add the spinach and paprika and cook, stirring, for 1–2 minutes, or until the leaves have just wilted.

4. Preheat the grill to medium–hot. Crack the eggs into a bowl and season to taste with salt and pepper, if using. Beat lightly with a fork until evenly mixed.

5. Pour a little extra oil into the pan if needed, then pour in the eggs and cook for 5–6 minutes, or until they are almost set and the underside of the frittata is golden brown.

6. Grill the frittata for 3–4 minutes, or until the top is browned and the eggs are set. Cut into wedges and serve immediately.

### WHY NOT TRY

*This versatile dish also makes a satisfying lunch or main meal. Serve with a crisp salad or steamed vegetables of your choice.*

# Egg White Omelette

*Separate the whites from the yolks to make this healthy breakfast omelette with peppers and goat's cheese, perfect by itself or as an accompaniment to a more hearty breakfast.*

| SERVES: | PREP: *20 mins* | | PER SERVING: *146 Kcals* | *9.4g fat* | *6.2g sat fat* | *3.7g carbs* | *1.8g sugar* |
|---|---|---|---|
| 1 | COOK: *12–14 mins* | | *1.3g fibre* | *11g protein* | *1.9g salt* |

## INGREDIENTS

*¼ red pepper, deseeded*
*2 large egg whites*
*1 spring onion, thinly sliced*
*pinch of salt*
*pinch of pepper*
*1 spray of vegetable or olive oil spray*
*30 g/1 oz fresh goat's cheese*
*2 tsp chopped fresh basil, plus extra sprigs*
  *to garnish*
*1 tbsp snipped fresh chives, to garnish*

1. Preheat the grill. Put the red pepper on a baking tray under the grill, skin-side up, and roast until it begins to blacken. Remove and place in a polythene bag or a bowl covered with clingfilm and set aside until cool enough to handle. Discard the blackened skin and dice the pepper.

2. In a small bowl, mix the egg whites, spring onion, salt and pepper together, stirring to combine well.

3. Coat a frying pan with the vegetable or olive oil spray and heat over a medium heat. Add the egg mixture and cook for about 3 minutes or until the egg is set, turning the frying pan frequently and running a palette knife around the edge to maintain a thin, even layer of egg.

4. Crumble the goat's cheese in a strip down the centre of the omelette, then top with the diced pepper and the basil. Fold the sides over the filling and slide the omelette onto a plate. Serve immediately, garnished with basil and chives.

## TRY SOMETHING DIFFERENT
*Replace the red pepper with sliced chestnut mushrooms.*
*Fry the mushrooms over a high heat for 5 minutes before adding to the cooked omelette with the goat's cheese.*

# Asparagus, Salmon & Poached Egg

*Perfect your poached egg skills and serve on top of a bed of salmon and asparagus for a light, fresh and delicious breakfast.*

| SERVES: | PREP: *20–25 mins, plus chilling* |
|---|---|
| 2 | COOK: *28–30 mins* |

**PER SERVING:** *702 Kcals | 52.4g fat | 19g sat fat | 6.3g carbs | 1.8g sugar 1.8g fibre | 52.6g protein | 3.7g salt*

## INGREDIENTS

*50 g/1¾ oz unsalted butter, softened*
*finely grated zest of ½ unwaxed lemon, plus*
  *½ tsp juice*
*sprig of fresh dill, roughly chopped*
*400 g/14 oz hot-smoked salmon*
*10 asparagus spears, woody stems removed*
*2 large eggs*
*sea salt and pepper (optional)*

1. Preheat the oven to 180°C/350°F/Gas Mark 4. Put the butter, lemon zest and juice and dill in a small bowl, season to taste with salt and pepper, if using and mix. Pat the butter into a rough square with the back of a spoon, wrap it in clingfilm and chill in the refrigerator while you make the rest of the dish.

2. Wrap the hot-smoked salmon in kitchen foil and bake for 15 minutes. Flake the fish into bite-sized pieces and keep warm.

3. Cook the asparagus in a large pan of lightly salted boiling water for 2 minutes. Drain and run under a cold tap briefly to stop the cooking process, then set aside.

4. Heat a wide saucepan of water until it is almost at simmering point. Crack one egg into a cup, then stir the water to make a whirlpool. As the whirlpool slows almost to a stop, gently slip the egg into its centre. Cook for 3½–4 minutes, then remove with a slotted spoon. Repeat with the second egg.

5. Put five asparagus spears on each of two plates, top with half the flaked salmon, then balance a poached egg on top and crown with a dab of lemon butter. Serve immediately.

**TOP TIP**

*The remaining heat from the egg should melt the lemon butter into a delicious lemon herb sauce.*

# Ham & Egg Cups

*These baked eggs look sophisticated but take just minutes to prepare, so breakfast can feel like a special meal any day of the week.*

| SERVES: | PREP: *20 mins* | PER SERVING: *160 Kcals* \| *11g fat* \| *4.3g sat fat* \| *1.7g carbs* \| *0.6g sugar* |
|---|---|---|
| 4 | COOK: *15–20 mins* | *0.5g fibre* \| *13.5g protein* \| *0.7g salt* |

### INGREDIENTS

*1 tbsp olive oil, for oiling*
*8 slices wafer-thin ham*
*15 g/½ oz butter*
*4 spring onions, thinly sliced*
*4 large hen eggs or duck eggs*
*pepper (optional)*
*4 slices hot buttered toast, to serve (optional)*

1. Preheat the oven to 200°C/400°F/Gas Mark 6. Lightly oil four holes in a muffin tin. Line each hole with 2 slices of ham, laying the slices across one another and ruffling them around the sides to make cups. There will be some ham protruding above the top of the tin.

2. Melt the butter in a small frying pan. Add the spring onions and gently fry for 2 minutes until soft. Remove from the heat. Divide two thirds of the onions and their buttery juice between the ham cups.

3. Crack the eggs one at a time into a small bowl. Slide into the ham cups, taking care not to let the eggs run down the sides. Season to taste with pepper, if using. Spoon over the remaining spring onions and bake in the preheated oven for 12–15 minutes until the whites of the eggs are just set. Serve immediately with hot buttered toast, if using.

### TRY SOMETHING DIFFERENT
*Replace the spring onions with a few thinly sliced and fried mushrooms, or spoon 1 teaspoon of tomato ketchup into the base of each ham cup and sprinkle the eggs with grated cheese before baking.*

# Poached Eggs & Kale with Sourdough

*Kale adds valuable nutrients and vivid green colour to these protein-packed poached eggs served on sensational sourdough toast.*

| SERVES: | PREP: *20 mins* | PER SERVING: *324 Kcals* | *15.1g fat* | *3g sat fat* | *36.3g carbs* | *2.6g sugar* |
|---|---|---|
| 4 | COOK: *18–20 mins* | *4.4g fibre* | *12.6g protein* | *1g salt* |

## INGREDIENTS

*4 eggs*
*100 g/3½ oz kale, chopped*
*4 large slices wholemeal sourdough bread*
*2 garlic cloves, chopped into halves*
*2 tbsp olive oil*
*1 tsp dried red chilli flakes*
*sea salt and pepper (optional)*

1. Begin by poaching the eggs. Bring a shallow saucepan of water to a gentle simmer. Crack an egg into a small bowl or ramekin, then slide the egg into the water, lowering the bowl as close to the water as possible. Using a large spoon, gently fold any stray strands of white around the yolk. Repeat with the other eggs.

2. Cook for 3½–4 minutes, or until set to your liking, then remove with a slotted spoon. Place the eggs in a small bowl of warm water so they can sit until needed.

3. Bring a saucepan of water to the boil and add the kale. Simmer for 3–4 minutes, or until the kale is just cooked but still retains a little crunch. Drain, season with salt and pepper, if using, and set aside.

4. Meanwhile, toast the sourdough bread. Place the toast on four plates, then rub each slice with the raw garlic and drizzle with the olive oil. Top the toast with the blanched kale and a poached egg. Finally, sprinkle over the chilli flakes. Serve immediately.

**WHY NOT TRY**

*If you don't have kale you could always use spinach for this recipe. It would also work well topped with scrambled eggs.*

# Know Your Eggs

The beauty of eggs is their versatility; however short of time you are they make a perfect and nutritious meal. Just follow a few simple rules and try to use fresh eggs as much as possible.

## MASTERING THE BASICS WITH HEN EGGS

### *Portion size: 2-3 eggs per person*

### SOFT- AND HARD-BOILED EGGS

Cook in fast boiling water for 3–4 minutes for soft boiled eggs. For hard boiled, cook in fast boiling water for 6–7 minutes, then run under cold water for 1 minute after cooking to prevent a dark ring from forming around the yolk.

### POACHED EGGS

3½–4 minutes. Do not add salt to the water. Add a little vinegar to help keep the egg whites together (about 3 tablespoons for each litre/1¾ pints of water). Cook the eggs in a sauté pan or frying pan, with about 7.5 cm/3 inches of water. To test if the egg is cooked, lift it out with a slotted spoon and very lightly press the egg with your fingertip. The white should be set and the yolk should feel soft. If cooking in advance or for a crowd, keep the poached eggs warm in a bowl of warm water – or cold water if using cold in salads. Drain well on clean kitchen paper before serving.

### OMELETTE

To make a classic folded omelette, simply whisk together 2–3 eggs with some seasoning until light and frothy. Add a little butter to a hot frying pan and when it is just beginning to brown add the eggs and stir briskly with a fork for 8–10 seconds until it begins to thicken. Using a spatula, move the setting egg at the sides of the pan into the centre and continue cooking for a further 15–30 seconds, or until lightly set. Place some cheese or ham into the centre of the omelette and continue cooking until the cheese has melted or the ham has sufficiently warmed through. Increase the heat slightly and cook for a further 30 seconds, until the omelette is fully set and browned on the bottom. Fold the omelette in half, slide onto a warmed plate and serve immediately.

### PAN-FRIED EGGS

Heat a non-stick frying pan with a little oil. Carefully break the egg into a cup and pour into the pan. This will help it to slide into the pan without breaking the yolk. Fry over a medium heat for 3–4 minutes until the egg white is firm but the yolk is still soft. If you prefer, flip the egg during cooking to fry both sides.

### SCRAMBLED EGGS

2 eggs will take 5–8 minutes; season well, whisk for 1 minute until frothy before cooking. Don't add salt until you're ready to cook, or the eggs will be rubbery in texture.

| COOKING TECHNIQUE | DUCK EGG | GOOSE EGG | QUAIL EGG |
|---|---|---|---|
| **PORTION SIZE** | 1 egg per person | 1 egg for 2-3 people | 2-3 eggs per person |
| **SOFT BOILED** | 6-7 minutes | 9-11 minutes | 30 seconds |
| **HARD BOILED** | 9 minutes | 13 minutes | 1 minute |
| **POACHED** | 5 minutes | 9-12 minutes | 30 seconds |
| **SCRAMBLED** | 6-9 minutes | 12-15 minutes | not recommended |

# Duck Eggs Benedict

*A delicious twist on the American classic, with crispy grilled pancetta and luxurious duck egg hollandaise sauce.*

| SERVES: | PREP: *20 mins* |
|---|---|
| 4 | COOK: *15 mins* |

PER SERVING: *389 Kcals | 28.4g fat | 12.4g sat fat | 15.7g carbs | 3.2g sugar 0.9g fibre | 17.1g protein | 1.7g salt*

## INGREDIENTS

*1 tsp white wine vinegar*
*4 fresh duck eggs*
*8 slices pancetta or dry-cure*
  *smoked streaky bacon rashers*
*2 English muffins*
*softened butter, for spreading (optional)*
*pepper (optional)*
*½ tsp snipped fresh chives, to garnish*

## HOLLANDAISE SAUCE

*1 duck egg yolk*
*2 tsp water*
*1 tsp lemon juice*
*55 g/2 oz butter, melted and cooled slightly*
*pinch of cayenne pepper*
*salt (optional)*

1. To make the hollandaise sauce, place the egg yolk, water and lemon juice in a heatproof bowl and whisk until pale and foamy. Place the bowl over a pan of barely simmering water and continue whisking for 1–2 minutes until the egg is slightly thickened.

2. Remove the bowl from the pan, then pour in the butter in a very thin stream, whisking continuously to make a light smooth sauce – stop pouring before you reach the milk solids in the base of the pan. Season to taste with salt, if using, and a pinch of cayenne pepper. Keep warm over the pan of hot water with the heat turned off until ready to serve.

3. Preheat the grill. Half fill a wide saucepan with water, heat until simmering, then add the vinegar. Crack the eggs into a cup one at a time and gently slide into the water. Poach for 5 minutes. Remove with a slotted spoon and drain on kitchen paper.

4. Meanwhile, grill the pancetta for 1–2 minutes until crispy and chop the slices in half. Split, toast and butter the muffins, if liked.

5. Place half a muffin on each plate, divide the grilled pancetta between them and season to taste with a little pepper, if using.

6. Top with the eggs, spoon about 2 tablespoons of the hollandaise sauce over each one and sprinkle with chives to garnish. Serve immediately.

# Chive Scrambled Eggs with Brioche

*As a slightly decadent twist on the usual scrambled eggs on toast, add chives and serve on brioche slices for an indulgent start to the day.*

| SERVES: | PREP: *10 mins* |
|---|---|
| 4 | COOK: *6–8 mins* |

PER SERVING: *269 Kcals* | *17.8g fat* | *9.2g sat fat* | *17g carbs* | *4.2g sugar* *0.6g fibre* | *9.7g protein* | *0.6g salt*

## INGREDIENTS

*4 eggs*
*100 ml/3½ fl oz single cream*
*2 tbsp snipped fresh chives*
*25 g/1 oz butter*
*4 slices brioche loaf, lightly toasted*
*salt and pepper (optional)*
*4 whole fresh chives, to garnish*

1. Break the eggs into a medium bowl and whisk gently with the cream. Season to taste with salt and pepper, if using and add the snipped chives.

2. Melt the butter in a sauté pan and pour in the egg mixture. Leave to set slightly, then move the mixture towards the centre of the pan using a wooden spoon as the eggs begin to cook. Continue in this way until the eggs are cooked but still creamy.

3. Place the toasted brioche slices on two warmed plates and spoon over the scrambled eggs. Serve immediately, garnished with whole chives.

**TRY SOMETHING DIFFERENT**
*For a healthier version swap the single cream for skimmed milk and the butter for cooking oil spray.*

# Polenta Cakes with Poached Eggs

*To use the polenta trimmings, chop roughly, place in a shallow ovenproof dish, brush with melted butter and grill for 3 minutes. Serve as an unusual side dish.*

| SERVES: | PREP: *20 mins, plus cooling* | PER SERVING: *429 Kcals* | *23.9g fat* | *11g sat fat* | *35g carbs* | *0.9g sugar* |
|---|---|---|
| 4 | COOK: *15–18 mins* | *3g fibre* | *18.2g protein* | *1.4g salt* |

## INGREDIENTS

*1 tbsp oil, for oiling*
*600 ml/1 pint water*
*150 g/5½ oz polenta*
*85 g/3 oz freshly grated Parmesan cheese*
*40 g/1½ oz butter*
*½ red chilli, deseeded and very finely chopped*
*200 g/7 oz baby spinach leaves, or a mixture of baby spinach leaves and rocket leaves*
*2 tsp white wine vinegar*
*4 large eggs*
*salt and pepper (optional)*

1. Lightly oil an 18-cm/7-inch square cake tin. Bring the water to the boil in a saucepan. Add the polenta in a thin stream and cook, stirring, over a medium–low heat for 3 minutes until thick. Stir in 55 g/2 oz of the cheese, 30 g/1 oz of the butter and the chilli.

2. Working quickly, transfer to the prepared tin and level the surface. Set aside for 30 minutes until cool and firm, then cut out four rounds with a 9-cm/3½-inch cutter and transfer to a baking tray.

3. Wash the spinach and place in a large saucepan with the water clinging to the leaves. Cover and cook for 2–3 minutes until wilted, then squeeze out the excess water between two plates. Return to the pan.

4. Preheat the grill to high. Sprinkle the polenta rounds with the remaining cheese, place under the preheated grill and cook for 3 minutes until brown and bubbling on the top. Keep warm. Meanwhile, add the remaining butter to the spinach and heat through.

5. Half fill a saucepan with water, add the vinegar and bring to simmering point. Crack the eggs into cups and slide gently into the water. Cook over a low heat, without allowing the water to boil, for 3½–4 minutes until the whites are firm and the yolk is still soft. Scoop out with a slotted spoon and drain briefly on kitchen paper.

6. To serve, place the polenta rounds on four warmed plates and divide the spinach between them. Top with the eggs and season to taste with salt and pepper, if using. Serve immediately.

# Mushroom & Egg Cups

*Here the classic flavours of breakfast – egg, bacon and mushroom – are combined in a more unusual, yet equally delicious, way.*

| SERVES: | PREP: *25 mins* | PER SERVING: *418 Kcals* | *18.1g fat* | *4.8g sat fat* | *49.5g carbs* | *3.7g sugar* |
|---|---|---|
| 6 | COOK: *20–25 mins* | *7.4g fibre* | *18.8g protein* | *1.9g salt* |

## INGREDIENTS

*2 tbsp virgin olive oil*
*2 oak-smoked back bacon rashers, rind*
*  removed, diced*
*115 g/4 oz button mushrooms, sliced*
*3 eggs*
*125 ml/4 fl oz milk*
*40 g/1½ oz Cheddar cheese, grated*
*1 tbsp finely snipped fresh chives*
*200 g/7 oz cherry tomatoes on the vine*
*sea salt and pepper (optional)*
*6 slices wholemeal bread, to serve*

1. Preheat the oven to 190°C/375°F/Gas Mark 5. Line the holes of a six-hole muffin tin with baking paper. Heat 1 tablespoon of oil in a small frying pan over a medium–high heat. Add the bacon and fry for 2–3 minutes, or until just beginning to turn golden. Add the mushrooms and fry, stirring, for 2 minutes. Spoon the mixture into the muffin tin holes.

2. Crack the eggs into a jug, add the milk, Cheddar and chives and season to taste with salt and pepper, if using. Beat lightly with a fork until evenly mixed, then pour into the holes of the muffin tin. Stir so the bacon and mushrooms are not all on the base of the tin. Bake in the centre of the oven for 15 minutes.

3. Put the tomatoes on a baking sheet, drizzle with the remaining oil and season to taste with salt and pepper, if using. Add to the oven for the last 10 minutes of cooking time. Lightly toast the bread, then cut each slice in half.

4. Lift out the mushroom and egg cups, arrange on plates with the toast and baked tomatoes and serve immediately.

## HELPFUL HINT

*Enjoy these baked eggs straight from the oven with hot wholemeal toast and baked tomatoes, or pack in foil with cherry tomatoes for a breakfast to go.*

# Tea–soaked Eggs

*These marinated eggs are a popular Chinese snack food traditionally served during the New Year celebrations. They make an interesting addition to rice and noodle dishes, salads, picnics and packed lunches.*

| MAKES: | PREP: *15 mins, plus standing & chilling* | PER EGG: *74 Kcals | 4.7g fat | 1.6g sat fat | 0.8g carbs | 0.5g sugar* |
|---|---|---|
| 6 | COOK: *20 mins* | *trace fibre | 6.4g protein | 0.4g salt* |

## INGREDIENTS

*6 eggs*
*600 ml/1 pint water*
*2 black tea bags*
*2 tbsp dark soy sauce*
*2 tsp soft light brown sugar*
*3 star anise*
*1 small cinnamon stick*
*1-cm/½-inch piece fresh ginger, peeled and roughly chopped*

1. Place the eggs in a saucepan just large enough to hold them in a single layer and cover with cold water. Bring to the boil, then remove from the heat. Cover the pan and leave to stand for 7 minutes. Remove the eggs with a slotted spoon and cool under running water.

2. Using the back of a teaspoon, gently tap the eggs all over to create small cracks in the shells, taking care not to break the membrane underneath.

3. Pour the measured water into the pan. Add the tea bags, soy sauce, sugar, star anise, cinnamon and ginger. Stir to dissolve the sugar, then return the eggs to the pan. Gently simmer for 15 minutes.

4. Remove from the heat and leave to cool, then transfer the eggs in their liquid to a bowl. Cover and refrigerate for at least 8 hours or overnight. Drain the eggs and carefully peel off the shells to reveal the pattern underneath.

**TOP TIP**
*If you prefer a stronger flavour, leave the eggs in the marinade for up to 48 hours.*

# Chorizo & Quail's Egg Toasts

*Quail's eggs may be smaller in size, but not in flavour. Pair with slices of chorizo for an interesting and flavoursome breakfast, an inventive variation on traditional eggs and bacon.*

| MAKES: | PREP: *15–20 mins* | PER EGG TOAST: *103 Kcals* | *3.8g fat* | *1g sat fat* | *12.5g carbs* | *0.7g sugar* |
|---|---|---|
| 12 | COOK: *10–14 mins* | *0.6g fibre* | *4.6g protein* | *0.5g salt* |

## INGREDIENTS

*12 slices French bread, sliced on the*
  *diagonal, about 0.5 cm/¼ inch thick*
*40 g/1½ oz cured, ready-to eat chorizo,*
  *cut into 12 thin slices*
*1 tbsp olive oil*
*12 quail's eggs*
*¼ tsp mild paprika, for dusting*
*salt and pepper (optional)*

1. Preheat the grill to high. Arrange the slices of bread on a baking sheet and grill until golden brown on both sides.

2. Cut or fold the chorizo slices to fit on the toasts and set aside.

3. Heat a thin layer of oil in a large frying pan over a medium heat until a cube of bread browns in 30 seconds. Break the eggs into the frying pan and fry, spooning the fat over the yolks, until the whites are set and the yolks are cooked to your liking.

4. Remove the fried eggs from the frying pan and drain on kitchen paper. Immediately transfer to the chorizo-topped toasts and dust with a pinch of paprika. Sprinkle with salt and pepper to taste, if using, and serve at once.

## TOP TIP

*Despite their delicate appearance, quail's eggs can be difficult to crack because of a relatively thick membrane under the shell. Have a pair of scissors handy to cut through the membrane as you break the egg into the frying pan.*

# Devilled Eggs

*Ideal as an appetizer at a party or simply as a snack, devilled eggs pack a whole host of delicious flavours into just a few mouthfuls.*

| MAKES: | PREP: *20–25 mins, plus cooling* |
|---|---|
| 16 | COOK: *15 mins* |

**PER DEVILLED EGG:** *84 Kcals | 6.6g fat | 1.5g sat fat | 1.7g carbs | 0.9g sugar 0.5g fibre | 4.3g protein | 0.2g salt*

## INGREDIENTS

*8 large eggs*
*2 whole canned or bottled pimientos del piquillo*
*16 stoned green Spanish olives*
*5 tbsp mayonnaise*
*8 drops hot pepper sauce*
*¼ tsp of cayenne pepper*
*salt and pepper (optional)*
*1 tsp Spanish paprika, to garnish*
*16 Little Gem lettuce leaves, to serve*

1. Put the eggs into a saucepan, cover with cold water and slowly bring to the boil. Reduce the heat to very low, cover and simmer gently for 10 minutes. Drain the eggs and place under cold running water until they are cold.

2. Crack the eggshells and remove. Halve the eggs lengthways. Carefully remove the yolks and place them in a sieve set over a bowl and rub through, then mash with a fork.

3. Place the pimientos on kitchen paper to dry well, then finely chop, reserving 16 small strips.

4. Finely chop half the olives. Halve the remaining olives.

5. Add the chopped pimientos and chopped olives to the mashed egg yolks. Add the mayonnaise, mix together well, then add the hot pepper sauce, cayenne pepper, and season to taste with salt and pepper, if using.

6. Use a teaspoon to spoon a little of the egg yolk mixture into the hollow in each egg white half.

7. Add a small strip of the reserved pimientos and an olive half to the top of each stuffed egg.

8. Line a platter with lettuce leaves and arrange the eggs on top. Dust with a little paprika and serve.

# Spicy Oven—baked Scotch Eggs

*These Scotch eggs are packed with flavour, but are lower in fat and simpler to prepare than the original picnic fare invented by London department store Fortnum & Mason.*

| SERVES: | PREP: *25 mins, plus standing & cooling* | PER SERVING: *353 Kcals* \| *23.2g fat* \| *7.2g sat fat* \| *16.2g carbs* \| *2.2g sugar* |
|---|---|---|
| 4 | COOK: *30 mins* | *1.2g fibre* \| *18.7g protein* \| *1.6g salt* |

## INGREDIENTS

*4 large eggs*

*1 tbsp oil, for oiling*

*300 g/10½ oz sausages, skins removed*

*1 tbsp mild curry paste*

*1 tsp onion seeds*

*2 tbsp roughly chopped fresh flat-leaf parsley leaves*

*55 g/2 oz fresh white breadcrumbs*

*2 tbsp milk*

*mango chutney, to serve (optional)*

1. Place the eggs in a saucepan and cover with cold water. Bring to the boil, then remove from the heat. Cover the pan and leave to stand for 6 minutes. Drain and cool under cold running water, then carefully peel off the shells.

2. Preheat the oven to 190°C/375°F/Gas Mark 5. Lightly oil a baking tray or line with non-stick baking paper. Place the sausage meat, curry paste, onion seeds and parsley in a bowl. Mix well. Add the breadcrumbs and milk and mix again. Divide into four equal portions.

3. Lay a piece of clingfilm on the work surface. Place a quarter of the sausage mixture on top and flatten with clean hands to a diameter of about 13 cm/5 inches. Place an egg in the centre and use the clingfilm to lift and mould the mixture around it. Smooth over the edges to seal. Place on the baking tray. Repeat with the remaining sausage mixture and eggs.

4. Bake in the preheated oven for 25 minutes until lightly browned. Serve hot or cold with the mango chutney, if liked.

### TRY SOMETHING DIFFERENT

*To make low-fat Scotch eggs, omit the spices at step 2 and roll the sausage-covered eggs in 55 g/2 oz dried breadcrumbs to coat. Place on a baking tray and drizzle each one with 1 teaspoon of olive oil before baking.*

# Perfect Pickled Eggs

*This traditional snack can easily be made at home. For this recipe you'll need a 1-litre/1¾ pint jar and this will allow space for 12 eggs.*

| SERVES: 12 | PREP: *15 mins, plus standing*<br>COOK: *20 mins* | PER EGG: *73 Kcals* \| *4.8g fat* \| *1.6g sat fat* \| *0.7g carbs* \| *0.5g sugar*<br>*0g fibre* \| *6.3g protein* \| *0.3g salt* |
|---|---|---|

## INGREDIENTS

*12 eggs*

*200 ml/7 fl oz distilled white vinegar*

*200 ml/7 fl oz water*

*1 tbsp sugar*

*2 tsp pickling spice*

*1 tsp cumin seeds*

*2 garlic cloves, peeled and crushed*

*1 tsp salt*

*12–14 pickled chillies, plus 100 ml/3½ fl oz of the juice from the jar*

1. Place the eggs in a saucepan and cover with cold water. Bring to the boil, then remove from the heat. Cover the pan and leave to stand for 10 minutes. Drain and cool under cold running water, then peel off the shells.

2. Place the vinegar, water, sugar, pickling spice, cumin, garlic and salt in a small saucepan. Bring to the boil, then reduce the heat, cover and simmer for 10 minutes.

3. Layer the eggs and chillies in a 1-litre/1¾-pint jar. Pour in the juice from the chilli jar and add the hot liquid and spices from the pan. Cover the jar and leave to cool until completely cold.

4. Store in the refrigerator and leave for at least 3 days before eating. Use within 1 month.

### HELPFUL HINT

*Don't limit these tangy treats to chips or a glass of beer! Try serving them as an accompaniment to deli meats and cheeses or chopped and sprinkled over grilled fish such as tuna steaks and sardines.*

# Lunch

BEETROOT & EGG SOUP 44

LENTIL & EGG SALAD 46

SPICY STUFFED SWEET POTATOES 49

BORLOTTI BEAN, TOMATO & EGG SALAD 50

EGGS BAKED IN AVOCADOS 53

THE BENEFITS OF EATING FREE-RANGE EGGS 55

CHICKEN & EGG ROLLS 56

ASPARAGUS & EGG PASTRIES 59

STEAMED GOOSE EGGS WITH BROAD BEANS 60

CROQUE MADAME 63

SALMON & DILL EGG WHITE QUICHE 64

SKINNY TURKEY & EGG SANDWICHES 66

EGGY BUBBLE & SQUEAK CAKES 69

# Beetroot & Egg Soup

*Eggs don't have to be enjoyed simply by themselves or in a cake! Try them in a soup and create a sumptuous dish perfect for lunch or as an impressive dinner party course.*

| SERVES: | PREP: *25 mins, plus cooling & chilling* | PER SERVING: *150 Kcals* \| *4.6g fat* \| *1.9g sat fat* \| *25.1g carbs* \| *20g sugar* |
|---|---|---|
| 6 | COOK: *25 mins* | *3.1g fibre* \| *6.4g protein* \| *2.6g salt* |

## INGREDIENTS

*650 g/1 lb 7 oz cooked beetroots,*
  *peeled and chopped*
*2 lemons, peeled, deseeded*
  *and chopped*
*1.3 litres/2¼ pints vegetable stock*
*3 large eggs*
*1½ tbsp clear honey, plus 2 tbsp extra for*
  *drizzling*
*pinch of salt*

## TO GARNISH (OPTIONAL)
*soured cream, chilled*
*snipped fresh chives*

1.  Put the beetroots and lemons into a large saucepan, pour in the stock and bring to the boil. Reduce the heat and simmer for 20 minutes.

2.  Remove the pan from the heat and leave to cool slightly. Ladle the soup into a food processor, in batches if necessary, and process to a purée. Pass the soup through a sieve into a bowl to remove any membrane or fibres. Leave to cool completely.

3.  Meanwhile, put the eggs, honey and a pinch of salt into a food processor and process until thoroughly combined. Gradually add the mixture to the soup, stirring constantly.

4.  Cover with clingfilm and chill in the refrigerator for at least 3 hours. To serve, stir the soup and taste and adjust the seasoning, if necessary. Ladle into bowls, drizzle with honey, garnish with the soured cream and snipped chives, if using, and serve.

### TRY SOMETHING DIFFERENT
*This chilled soup is perfect for a warm summer day.*
*Serve as an alfresco lunch with a crunchy salad, fresh*
*cheese and crusty bread.*

# Lentil & Egg Salad

*Salads needn't only be enjoyed when the weather is hot. This robust, earthy lentil salad can be rustled up quickly after work and, as it is served just-warm, makes a great dish for cooler autumn days.*

| SERVES: | PREP: *20–25 mins, plus cooling* | | PER SERVING: *383 Kcals* | *16.9g fat* | *3.9g sat fat* | *37.1g carbs* | *1.9g sugar* |
|---|---|---|---|
| 4 | COOK: *40 mins* | | *18g fibre* | *22g protein* | *2.6g salt* |

## INGREDIENTS

*850 ml/1½ pints vegetable stock*
*2 bay leaves*
*1 cinnamon stick, halved*
*225 g/8 oz leeks*
*225 g/8 oz green lentils, rinsed and drained*
*3 tbsp olive oil*
*2 garlic cloves, finely chopped*
*4 eggs*
*2 tbsp capers, drained and chopped*
*85 g/3 oz baby spinach*
*25 g/1 oz fresh flat-leaf parsley, roughly chopped, to garnish*

## DRESSING

*2 tbsp red wine vinegar*
*1 tsp Dijon mustard*
*salt and pepper (optional)*

1. Put the stock, bay leaves and cinnamon in a saucepan and bring just to the boil. Cut a 7.5-cm/3-inch piece from the white base of one of the leeks and add this and the lentils to the pan. Cover and simmer for 25 minutes, or until the lentils are tender and nearly all of the stock has been absorbed. Top up with a little boiling water during cooking if needed. Drain the lentils, transfer to a salad bowl and discard the cooked leek, bay leaves and cinnamon stick.

2. Meanwhile, thinly slice the rest of the leeks. Heat 1 tablespoon of olive oil in a frying pan over a medium heat. Add the leeks and the garlic and fry for 3–4 minutes, stirring, until just beginning to soften. Remove from the heat and leave to cool.

3. Put the eggs in a saucepan and pour in enough cold water to cover them by 1 cm/½ inch. Bring to the boil, then reduce the heat and boil for 8 minutes. Drain immediately, cool quickly under cold running water, then peel and cut into quarters.

4. To make the dressing, put the vinegar, remaining 2 tablespoons of oil and the mustard in a jam jar, season to taste with salt and pepper, if using, screw on the lid and shake well. Drizzle over the lentils and toss gently together.

5. Top with the sliced leeks, capers and spinach. Arrange the hard-boiled eggs over the salad, sprinkle with the parsley and serve warm.

# Spicy Stuffed Sweet Potatoes

*A comforting lunch or brunch dish ideal for chilly autumn and winter days. Chorizo varies in flavour from smoky to hot and spicy, in which case you may want to leave out the extra chilli!*

| SERVES: | PREP: *20 mins, plus cooling* |
|---|---|
| 4 | COOK: *1 hr 5 mins–1 hr 15 mins* |

**PER SERVING:** *369 Kcals | 15.4g fat | 5.4g sat fat | 43.4g carbs | 9.7g sugar 6.6g fibre | 14.3g protein | 1.7g salt*

## INGREDIENTS

*2 similar-sized sweet potatoes,
  375–400 g/13–14 oz each*
*1 tbsp olive oil, plus 1 tbsp extra for oiling*
*1 small onion, chopped*
*55 g/2 oz chorizo, chopped into small pieces*
*1 red chilli, deseeded and finely chopped
  (optional)*
*1 garlic clove, crushed*
*30 g/1 oz mature Cheddar cheese, finely
  grated*
*3 tbsp roughly chopped fresh coriander, plus
  extra to garnish*
*4 small eggs*
*salt and pepper (optional)*

1.  Preheat the oven to 200°C/400°F/Gas Mark 6. Oil a baking tray. Place the sweet potatoes on the prepared tray and bake in the preheated oven for 50 minutes–1 hour until cooked through in the centre. Set aside for 15 minutes until cool enough to handle.

2.  Meanwhile, heat the oil in a frying pan, add the onion, chorizo, and chilli, if using. Cook over a low heat for 7–8 minutes, stirring occasionally, until the onions are tender and beginning to brown. Add the garlic and cook, stirring, for a further minute.

3.  Slice the potatoes in half lengthways and scoop most of the flesh from the centres, leaving a layer around the sides so the thin skins do not collapse. Transfer the flesh to a bowl and mash, then stir in the fried onion mixture, cheese and coriander.

4.  Pile the mash back into the potato halves and place on the baking tray. Make a hollow in the top of each one and carefully break in an egg. Season with salt and pepper, if using. Return to the oven for 15 minutes until the eggs have just set. Sprinkle with coriander and serve immediately.

### TOP TIP

*The sweet potato cases can be cooked and filled the evening or morning before you need them, and stored in the refrigerator. Heat through in the oven for a few minutes before cracking in the eggs.*

# Borlotti Bean, Tomato & Egg Salad

*If you think salads are tasteless and unsatisfying, then think again! Adding hard-boiled eggs provide them with a heartier edge, and this recipe is no exception.*

| SERVES: | PREP: *20–25 mins, plus soaking* | PER SERVING: *492 Kcals* \| *26.1g fat* \| *4.5g sat fat* \| *45.4g carbs* \| *3.2g sugar* |
|---------|----------------------------------|------------------------------------------------------------------------------------------|
| 4 | COOK: *1 hr 45 mins–2 hrs 15 mins* | *16.8g fibre* \| *21.9g protein* \| *1.7g salt* |

## INGREDIENTS

*250 g/9 oz dried borlotti beans, soaked in
  cold water for several hours*
*2 large garlic cloves, crushed*
*juice of 2 lemons*
*6 tbsp extra virgin olive oil*
*1 tsp salt*
*1 small onion, finely diced*
*2 tomatoes, deseeded and finely diced*
*40 g/1½ oz fresh flat-leaf parsley, thick
  stems removed, leaves chopped*
*1 tsp cumin seeds, crushed*
*4 hard-boiled eggs, quartered*
*pepper (optional)*

## TO GARNISH

*4 lemon wedges*
*sumac (optional)*

1. Drain the beans, rinse well and put into a large saucepan. Cover with water and bring to the boil. Boil for 10 minutes, then reduce the heat and simmer for 1½–2 hours, or until very tender. Top up with boiling water if necessary.

2. Drain the beans and tip into a shallow serving dish. Lightly crush some of them with the back of a wooden spoon.

3. Add the garlic, lemon juice, olive oil and salt while the beans are still warm. Mix gently, then add the onion, tomatoes and parsley.

4. Add the cumin seeds and some pepper, if using, and gently toss.

5. Arrange the egg quarters and lemon wedges on top. Sprinkle with a pinch of sumac, if using, and serve.

**WHY NOT TRY**

*If you don't have sumac, try sprinkling with crushed red
pepper flakes instead.*

# Eggs Baked in Avocados

*The idea of eating hot avocado might seem strange, but the combination of creamy flesh, salty bacon and soft-cooked egg is perfect here.*

| SERVES: | PREP: *20 mins* | PER SERVING: *277 Kcals* \| *23.6g fat* \| *5.2g sat fat* \| *9.1g carbs* \| *0.8g sugar* |
|---|---|---|
| 4 | COOK: *20 mins* | *6.8g fibre* \| *10.2g protein* \| *0.8g salt* |

## INGREDIENTS

*5 streaky bacon rashers*
*2 large ripe avocados*
*4 small eggs*
*pepper (optional)*
*hot toast or salsa, to serve (optional)*

1. Preheat the oven to 220°C/425°F/Gas Mark 7 and the grill to high. Grill the bacon under the preheated grill for 5–6 minutes until crispy, then roughly chop.

2. Halve the avocados and remove the stones. Scoop out enough flesh to make a hole big enough to hold one egg. Place cut-side up on a bun tin or muffin tray – the dips in the tray will prevent them tilting over.

3. Drop 3–4 pieces of bacon into the base of each avocado. Crack an egg into a cup. To make sure the egg doesn't slide out of the avocado when you pour it in, scoop out the egg yolk with a spoon and drop it into the hole, then whisk the egg white lightly with a fork to break it up, then pour in enough to fill up the hole.

4. Repeat with the remaining eggs and season to taste with pepper, if using. Bake in the preheated oven for 15 minutes until the whites of the eggs are just set. Sprinkle with the remaining bacon and serve immediately with hot toast, or salsa, if liked.

### HELPFUL HINT
*Make an easy salsa with the leftover scooped-out avocado. Chop the avocado and two large ripe tomatoes and 1 small red onion. Place in a food processor with 2 tablespoons of lemon juice, 1 tablespoon of chopped fresh coriander and ¼ teaspoon of chilli powder. Blend until finely chopped.*

# The Benefits of Eating Free-Range Eggs

There are several different options when it comes to buying eggs in the supermarket but the overall opinion is that free-range eggs are the best. There are many factors that support this theory and it is not just because this is the most natural way that hens would live, there are health benefits too.

Hens are gregarious creatures. In the wild they would live in a flock with a natural hierarchy or 'pecking order'. During the day they would forage for food, scratching and searching, have regular dust baths to replenish the oils in their feathers and only seek shelter to cluster together at night in trees or under cover for roosting.

The best eggs come from chickens that are allowed to pasture and roam freely and eat a diet of plants and insects. The term 'free range' means that the eggs come from hens that have access to the outdoors, and have a natural and healthy diet, as opposed to barn-reared hens, which are confined to an indoor environment and a diet of grain and soya.

Unsurprisingly, hens that spend part or all their days foraging in the outdoors will be happier and healthier than those kept in barns, so choosing free-range eggs whenever possible is sensible. Free-range birds are housed in barns overnight to roost but they have more space to roam in daylight hours and will spend at least some of their time outdoors.

Organic hens have the ultimate lifestyle, enjoying even more living space, and they forage on land that has been certified organic. The flock sizes are smaller to encourage better welfare and their diet is organically produced. Colourings that artificially darken the egg yolks are banned.

The nutritional benefits of eating free-range eggs are dramatic. The hens' access to more grass and plants is reflected in the eggs themselves. In general the yolks from free-range hens are more golden in colour (although this can also depend on their diet), which gives a lovely rich colour to cakes and sauces.

Generally, free-range eggs have higher levels of omega 3, vitamins A, E and D and lower levels of total fat, saturated fat and cholesterol and omega 6. Interestingly, vitamin D, which is commonly deficient in many people, can be obtained only from direct sunlight on the skin or from a small list of foods. Eggs are also a really good source of vitamin D.

So, for the best taste, appearance and health benefits – as well as higher welfare for the hens– it has to be free-range, or organic, eggs every time.

# Chicken & Egg Rolls

*Delicious straight from the pan or cold at work, the range of flavours here will satisfy your hunger. You'll need metal skewers for this recipe to cook the chicken under the grill.*

| SERVES: 6 | PREP: *40 mins, plus marinating & resting*<br>COOK: *25–30 mins* | PER SERVING: *304 Kcals* \| *10.5g fat* \| *2.6g sat fat* \| *29.2g carbs* \| *1.5g sugar*<br>*1.4g fibre* \| *21.9g protein* \| *2.2g salt* |
| --- | --- | --- |

## INGREDIENTS

*2 skinless, boneless chicken breasts, cut into bite-sized pieces*
*200 g/7 oz plain flour, plus 1 tbsp for dusting*
*1 tsp salt*
*1 tbsp vegetable oil*
*100 ml/3½ fl oz milk*
*4 eggs*
*fresh mint leaves and sliced red onion, to serve (optional)*

## MARINADE

*2 garlic cloves, crushed*
*1 tsp grated fresh ginger*
*2 tsp ground cumin*
*1 tsp chilli powder*
*¼ tsp ground turmeric*
*¼ tsp garam masala*
*2 tsp tomato purée*
*2 tbsp wholemilk natural yogurt*
*1 tbsp lemon juice*
*1 tsp salt*
*1 tbsp vegetable oil*

1. Place all the marinade ingredients in a non-metallic bowl with the chicken and stir to mix well. Cover and chill in the refrigerator for 6–8 hours, or overnight if possible.

2. When ready to cook, preheat the grill to medium–high. Thread the marinated chicken onto metal skewers. Place the chicken skewers on a grill rack and cook under the preheated grill, turning once, for 12–15 minutes, until cooked through and tender. Remove the chicken from the skewers and keep warm.

3. Meanwhile, sift the flour and salt into a large bowl. Add the oil, milk and one of the eggs and knead for 8–10 minutes, until smooth. Form into a ball, cover and leave to rest for 15–20 minutes.

4. Divide the dough into six equal-sized pieces and form each into a ball. On a lightly floured surface, roll each ball into a round that is 16–17 cm/6¼–6½ inches in diameter and about 3 mm/⅛ inch thick. Lightly beat the remaining eggs.

5. Heat a non-stick frying pan over a medium heat. Working one at a time, place a dough round in the pan and cook for 1 minute. Flip it over and spread 1 tablespoon of the beaten egg all over the surface. Immediately flip it over again and cook for 30–40 seconds, then remove from the heat. Repeat until all the dough rounds have been cooked.

6. Divide the chicken between the egg rolls and scatter over a few mint leaves and some sliced red onion, if liked. Roll tightly to enclose the filling and serve.

# Asparagus & Egg Pastries

*These pastries make a delicious light lunch and spicy smoked paprika is the perfect addition to these baked eggs and asparagus.*

| SERVES: | PREP: *20 mins, plus chilling* |
|---|---|
| 4 | COOK: *25–30 mins* |

PER SERVING: *613 Kcals | 36.1g fat | 16.8g sat fat | 54.2g carbs | 5.9g sugar 5.1g fibre | 16.5g protein | 1.7g salt*

## INGREDIENTS

*500 g/1 lb 2 oz ready-made puff pastry*

*2 tbsp flour, for dusting*

*2 tbsp milk, for brushing*

*300 g/10½ oz slim asparagus spears*

*200 g/7 oz ready-made tomato pasta sauce*

*1 tsp hot smoked paprika*

*4 eggs*

*salt and pepper (optional)*

1. Roll out the pastry on a lightly floured surface to a 35 x 20-cm/14 x 8-inch rectangle, then cut into four pieces to make four 20 x 9-cm/8 x 3½-inch rectangles.

2. Line a baking tray with non-stick baking paper and place the pastry rectangles on the tray. Prick all over with a fork and brush lightly with milk. Chill for 20 minutes.

3. Snap the woody ends off the asparagus and discard. Bring a saucepan of lightly salted water to the boil, then add the asparagus, bring back to the boil and cook for 2–3 minutes until almost tender. Drain and refresh in cold water, then drain again.

4. Meanwhile, preheat the oven to 200°C/400°F/Gas Mark 6. Mix the tomato sauce and paprika together and divide between the pastry bases, spreading it out almost to the edges. Bake in the preheated oven for 10–12 minutes until the pastry is puffed around the edges and pale golden in colour.

5. Remove from the oven and top with the asparagus, leaving space for the egg in the middle of each pastry. Crack one egg into a cup and slide into the space created in one of the pastries.

6. Repeat with the remaining eggs, then return the pastries to the oven for 8 minutes, or until the eggs are just set. Season to taste with salt and pepper, if using, and serve immediately.

# Steamed Goose Eggs with Broad Beans

*A dish for spring and early summer, when goose eggs are in season, and home-grown beans and herbs are at their best.*

| SERVES: | PREP: *20–25 mins* |
|---|---|
| 2 | COOK: *25 mins* |

PER SERVING: *552 Kcals | 42g fat | 11.8g sat fat | 8.5g carbs | 2.1g sugar 3.4g fibre | 32.6g protein | 2.7g salt*

## INGREDIENTS

*100 g/3½ oz fresh or frozen broad beans*
*85 g/3 oz smoked bacon lardons*
*4 tsp olive oil*
*2 goose eggs*
*225 ml/8 fl oz chicken stock or vegetable stock*
*4 tbsp torn fresh basil leaves*
*2 tsp lemon juice*
*2 tsp water*
*pepper (optional)*

1. Bring a saucepan of water to the boil, add the beans and cook for 3 minutes. Drain and rinse under cold running water. Pop the beans out of their skins and discard the skins. Place the lardons in a non-stick frying pan with 1 teaspoon of the oil. Cook over a high heat until the fat runs off, then fry for 2 minutes until lightly browned. Remove from the heat then stir in the beans.

2. Lightly whisk the eggs and stock together with a fork and season to taste with pepper, if using. Stir in half the basil. Pour half the mixture into a 850-ml/1½-pint heatproof dish, such as a small pie dish, and scatter with one third of the beans and bacon.

3. Place the dish on a piece of scrunched foil in a deep frying pan, so that the dish is raised at least 2.5 cm/1 inch from the base. Pour in boiling water up to the base of the dish, cover the pan with a lid and steam for 5 minutes until the eggs are almost set in the middle.

4. Remove the dish from the pan. Pour in the remaining egg mixture and sprinkle with half the remaining bacon and beans. Carefully cover the top of the dish with clingfilm and steam for a further 10 minutes until just set and slightly wobbly in the middle.

5. Scatter the steamed eggs with the remaining bacon, beans and basil. Season to taste with pepper, if using. Whisk the remaining oil with lemon juice and water and drizzle over the top. Serve immediately.

# Croque Madame

*Baking the sandwiches works as well as grilling or pan-frying, and if you're making them for more than two people this method is much easier to manage. Top with the traditional fried egg if you prefer.*

| SERVES: | PREP: *15 mins* |
|---|---|
| 4 | COOK: *10–12 mins* |

PER SERVING: *619 Kcals* | *33.9g fat* | *11.9g sat fat* | *38.5g carbs* | *4.9g sugar*
*6.1g fibre* | *36.6g protein* | *3.6g salt*

## INGREDIENTS
*8 slices multigrain bread*
*40 g/1½ oz butter or reduced-fat spread*
*140 g/5 oz Gruyère cheese, grated*
*150 g/5½ oz sliced cooked ham*
*1 tsp white wine vinegar*
*4 large hen eggs or duck eggs*
*salt and pepper (optional)*
*rocket and red onion salad, to serve*

1. Preheat the oven to 230°C/450°F/Gas Mark 8. Spread the bread with butter and place four slices on a baking tray, buttered side down. Top with half the cheese, followed by the ham and then the remaining cheese.

2. Cover with the remaining slices of bread, buttered side up. Bake in the preheated oven for 10–12 minutes until golden brown and the cheese has melted, flipping them over using a fish slice or palette knife halfway through.

3. Meanwhile half-fill a wide saucepan with water. Add the vinegar and heat until barely simmering. Crack an egg into a cup and slide it into the water. Repeat with the remaining eggs and poach for 2–3 minutes until the whites are set and the yolks are still soft.

4. Remove from the pan with a slotted spoon and drain on absorbent kitchen paper. Top each sandwich with an egg and season to taste with salt and pepper, if using. Serve immediately with rocket and red onion salad.

### WHY NOT TRY
*To make a simple rocket salad simply whisk together 2 tablespoons of olive oil, 1 tablespoon of lemon juice, 1 tablespoon of cold water and some seasoning in a small bowl. Pour it over 40 g/1½ oz rocket and 1 small, very thinly sliced red onion. Toss together.*

# Croque Madame

Baking the sandwiches works as well as grilling or pan-frying, and if you're making them for more than two people this method is much easier to manage. Top with the traditional fried egg if you prefer.

| SERVES: | PREP: *15 mins* |
|---|---|
| 4 | COOK: *10–12 mins* |

PER SERVING: *619 Kcals | 33.9g fat | 11.9g sat fat | 38.5g carbs | 4.9g sugar 6.1g fibre | 36.6g protein | 3.6g salt*

## INGREDIENTS

*8 slices multigrain bread*
*40 g/1½ oz butter or reduced-fat spread*
*140 g/5 oz Gruyère cheese, grated*
*150 g/5½ oz sliced cooked ham*
*1 tsp white wine vinegar*
*4 large hen eggs or duck eggs*
*salt and pepper (optional)*
*rocket and red onion salad, to serve*

1. Preheat the oven to 230°C/450°F/Gas Mark 8. Spread the bread with butter and place four slices on a baking tray, buttered side down. Top with half the cheese, followed by the ham and then the remaining cheese.

2. Cover with the remaining slices of bread, buttered side up. Bake in the preheated oven for 10–12 minutes until golden brown and the cheese has melted, flipping them over using a fish slice or palette knife halfway through.

3. Meanwhile half-fill a wide saucepan with water. Add the vinegar and heat until barely simmering. Crack an egg into a cup and slide it into the water. Repeat with the remaining eggs and poach for 2–3 minutes until the whites are set and the yolks are still soft.

4. Remove from the pan with a slotted spoon and drain on absorbent kitchen paper. Top each sandwich with an egg and season to taste with salt and pepper, if using. Serve immediately with rocket and red onion salad.

### WHY NOT TRY

*To make a simple rocket salad simply whisk together 2 tablespoons of olive oil, 1 tablespoon of lemon juice, 1 tablespoon of cold water and some seasoning in a small bowl. Pour it over 40 g/1½ oz rocket and 1 small, very thinly sliced red onion. Toss together.*

# Salmon & Dill Egg White Quiche

*The dill perfectly complements the salmon in this tempting quiche, ideal as a light dinner on a summer's evening.*

| SERVES: | PREP: *20 mins* |
|---------|-----------------|
| 6 | COOK: *50 mins, plus standing* |

PER SERVING: *156 Kcals* | *7.8g fat* | *2.3g sat fat* | *4.5g carbs* | *3.7g sugars* *0.8g fibre* | *16.5g protein* | *0.9g salt*

## INGREDIENTS

*275 g/9¾ oz skinless salmon fillet*
*2 courgettes, thinly sliced*
*7 egg whites*
*200 ml /7 fl oz milk*
*2 spring onions, thinly sliced*
*1 tbsp chopped fresh dill*
*3 tbsp freshly grated Parmesan cheese*
*salt and pepper (optional)*
*2 tbsp chopped fresh dill, to garnish*
  *(optional)*

1. Bring a wide saucepan of water to the boil. Reduce to a gentle simmer, then add the salmon and poach for 6–8 minutes, depending on the thickness of the fish, until just cooked through and the flesh flakes in the centre. Drain and flake into chunky pieces.

2. Meanwhile, preheat a dry griddle pan, add the courgettes and cook for about 8 minutes, turning once until cooked through and lightly charred on both sides.

3. Preheat the oven to 180°C/350°F/Gas Mark 4. Line a 20–23-cm/8–9-inch round baking dish with a piece of non-stick baking paper large enough to come up the sides. Gently whisk together the egg whites, milk and spring onions in a large, grease-free bowl.

4. Cover the prepared baking dish with half the salmon and courgette slices and season to taste with salt and pepper, if using. Sprinkle with half the dill and pour over half the egg mixture.

5. Repeat the layers, then sprinkle the top evenly with Parmesan cheese. Bake in the preheated oven for 35–40 minutes until lightly browned and just set in the middle. Leave to stand for 15 minutes before lifting from the dish using the paper.

6. Lightly grill the top if you prefer a browner finish. Serve warm or cold, garnished with chopped fresh dill, if using.

# Skinny Turkey & Egg Sandwiches

*This sandwich, made with healthy turkey, wholegrain bread and low-fat cheese, looks and tastes so great you will forget it's low fat! Enjoy with lots of peppery rocket leaves.*

| SERVES: | PREP: *20 mins* |
|---|---|
| 2 | COOK: *10–14 mins* |

PER SERVING: *475 Kcals* | *10.3g fat* | *3.2g sat fat* | *59.3g carbs* | *8.9g sugar* *7.8g fibre* | *37.7g protein* | *2.1g salt*

## INGREDIENTS

*½ red onion, peeled and sliced into whole rounds*
*2 thin turkey steaks or escalopes, about 90–100 g/3¼–3½ oz each*
*½ tsp all-purpose seasoning*
*¼ tsp smoked paprika*
*4 thick slices wholegrain bread*
*55 g/2 oz low-fat soft cheese*
*2 hard-boiled eggs, whites only, chopped*
*2 tomatoes, thinly sliced*
*1 lemon wedge*
*15 g/½ oz rocket leaves*
*salt and pepper (optional)*

1. Preheat a ridged griddle pan until smoking hot. Add the onion rounds and cook for 2–3 minutes on each side until soft and lightly charred. Transfer to a plate.

2. Wipe the turkey steaks with kitchen paper. Sprinkle with the all-purpose seasoning and paprika and rub into the meat. Arrange on the pan and cook for 3 minutes without moving them, until lightly charred underneath. Turn and cook for 2–3 minutes on the other side, until thoroughly cooked through.

3. Spread the bread with the soft cheese. Cover two slices with the chopped egg white and tomato slices. Cut the turkey steaks in half, arrange on top and squeeze over a little lemon juice.

4. Divide the rocket leaves between the sandwiches and season to taste with salt and pepper, if using. Top with the remaining bread, cut in half and serve immediately.

## TRY SOMETHING DIFFERENT

*For something different try lightly toasting the wholegrain bread before assembling the sandwich. You could also omit the top slice of bread and serve as an open sandwich.*

# Eggy Bubble & Squeak Cakes

*These patties are a great way of using up leftover vegetables, and 'hiding' ones which children wouldn't otherwise try! Try serving them as a side to sausages, ham or smoked fish dishes.*

| MAKES: | PREP: *25 mins, plus cooling* |
|---|---|
| 8 | COOK: *46–53 mins* |

PER CAKE: *115 Kcals* | *6.3g fat* | *1.6g sat fat* | *8.8g carbs* | *2.1g sugar*
*1.5g fibre* | *6g protein* | *0.6g salt*

## INGREDIENTS

*115 g/4 oz floury potatoes, cut into chunks*
*5 large eggs*
*1 tbsp olive oil, plus extra for frying*
*1 small onion, chopped*
*1 garlic clove, crushed*
*250 g/9 oz cooked vegetables, such as sprouts,*
  *swede, cabbage or parsnip, roughly chopped*
*1 tsp English mustard*
*5 tbsp fine dry breadcrumbs*
*salt and pepper (optional)*
*tomato ketchup, to serve (optional)*

1. Place the potatoes in a saucepan and cover with water, bring to the boil, then reduce the heat and simmer for 20–25 minutes until tender. Drain and stir over the heat for 30–60 seconds, then mash.

2. Meanwhile, place four of the eggs in a saucepan, cover with water and bring to the boil. Simmer for 7 minutes, drain, then cool under cold running water. Peel and roughly chop the eggs.

3. Heat the oil in a large non-stick frying pan. Add the onion and gently fry for 3–4 minutes until soft, then stir in the garlic and add the cooked vegetables. Spread out over the base of the pan and fry for a further 3–4 minutes without stirring, until brown underneath. Remove from the heat.

4. Transfer to a large bowl. Add the potatoes and chopped egg. Season to taste with salt and pepper, if using. Beat the remaining egg with the mustard, add to the bowl and mix well. Divide the mixture into eight equal portions and shape each portion into an 8-cm/3¼-inch round patty.

5. Place the breadcrumbs on a plate. Press the patties into them to cover both sides. Wipe out the frying pan. Add 1 teaspoon of oil and heat. Add four patties and fry for about 3 minutes until golden brown underneath. Turn, add another teaspoon of oil and fry for a further 3 minutes. Remove from the pan and keep warm while cooking the remaining patties in the same way. Serve immediately with tomato ketchup.

### TOP TIP
*Add just enough oil to brown the patties.*
*Doing so prevents the eggs from soaking up too much*
*oil and possibly exploding when placed over a high heat.*

# Mains

BARLEY & ASPARAGUS RISOTTO WITH POACHED EGG 73

COURGETTE FRITTERS WITH POACHED EGGS 74

WHOLEWHEAT SPINACH, PEA & FETA TART 77

ARTICHOKE & RED PEPPER TORTILLA 78

HAM & EGG PIE 81

HOW TO BUY THE BEST EGGS & KEEP THEM FRESH 83

FIORENTINA PIZZA 84

LONDON BURGERS 86

TOMATO & CARAMELIZED ONION STRATA 89

EGG & LENTIL CURRY 90

SKINNY CARBONARA 93

MEATLOAF STUFFED WITH QUAIL'S EGGS 94

STEAK TARTARE 97

EGG, MEATBALL & TOMATO TAGINE 98

# Barley & Asparagus Risotto with Poached Egg

*A dish to make in spring when goose eggs and asparagus are both in season. Humble pearl barley makes a creamy and delicious risotto. It takes longer to cook than risotto rice but requires much less stirring.*

| SERVES: | PREP: *20–25 mins* |
|---|---|
| 6 | COOK: *1 hr 30 mins* |

PER SERVING: *529 Kcals | 25.3g fat | 8.8g sat fat | 47.8g carbs | 5.1g sugar 9.4g fibre | 27g protein | 2g salt*

## INGREDIENTS

*30 g/1 oz butter*
*1 large onion, finely chopped*
*1 celery stick, finely chopped*
*2 garlic cloves, crushed*
*2 chicken stock cubes*
*1.6 litres /2¾ pints boiling water*
*300 g/10½ oz pearl barley*
*150 ml/5 fl oz dry cider*
*250 g/9 oz asparagus, trimmed*
*1 tsp white wine vinegar*
*6 goose (or duck) eggs*
*40 g/1½ oz low-fat soft cheese*
*115 g/4 oz freshly grated Parmesan cheese*
*pepper (optional)*

1. Heat the butter in a large saucepan until melted and foaming. Add the onion, celery and garlic. Cover and cook over a low heat for 10 minutes until the onion looks translucent. Meanwhile, dissolve the stock cubes in 850 ml/1½ pints of the boiling water.

2. Add the barley to the pan and stir to coat in the buttery juices. Pour in the cider and boil rapidly until most of the liquid has evaporated. Pour in the stock and simmer for 1 hour, stirring occasionally and adding the remaining boiling water as necessary after 30 minutes.

3. Meanwhile, steam the asparagus for 3–4 minutes, or until tender. Lift out with a slotted spoon and refresh in iced water, then drain and chop.

4. When the risotto is almost cooked, half fill a wide saucepan with water, add the vinegar and heat until simmering. Crack the eggs one at a time into a cup, then slide them into the water. Poach for 9 minutes until the whites are just set. Lift out with a slotted spoon and drain on absorbent kitchen paper.

5. Stir the soft cheese into the risotto until melted. Season to taste with pepper, if using. Add the asparagus and heat through for 1 minute, then stir in half the Parmesan cheese.

6. To serve, ladle the risotto into bowls and top with the poached eggs. Season to taste with pepper, if using, and sprinkle with the remaining Parmesan cheese.

# Courgette Fritters with Poached Eggs

*Pairing courgette fritters with a poached egg is a perfect idea for a quick, nourishing dinner after a long day, and the caramelized onions offer a subtle sweetness!*

| SERVES: | PREP: *25 mins, plus cooling* | PER SERVING: *564 Kcals* \| *28.8g fat* \| *5.4g sat fat* \| *59.6g carbs* \| *14.9g sugar* |
|---|---|---|
| 4 | COOK: *1 hr* | *4.7g fibre* \| *17g protein* \| *1.8g salt* |

## INGREDIENTS

*2 tbsp extra virgin olive oil*

*5 red onions, sliced*

*1 tbsp soft brown sugar*

*200 g/7 oz self-raising flour*

*1 egg, lightly beaten, plus 4 eggs for poaching*

*200 ml/7 fl oz milk*

*2 courgettes, grated*

*225 ml/8 fl oz sunflower oil*

*salt and pepper (optional)*

*1.* Heat the olive oil in a large heavy-based saucepan over a medium heat, add the onions and cook for 5 minutes, or until softened. Stir in the sugar and reduce the heat, cover and cook for 30 minutes, or until the onions are deep brown in colour, stirring occasionally. Season to taste with salt and pepper, if using, and leave to cool.

*2.* To make the fritters, place the flour in a large bowl and make a well in the centre. Whisk the beaten egg and milk together, then use a wooden spoon to incorporate into the flour. Season to taste with salt and pepper, if using, and stir in the grated courgettes.

*3.* Heat the sunflower oil in a wide deep-sided pan and drop in tablespoons of the batter. Cook, in batches if necessary, until golden brown on both sides, turning once. Drain on kitchen paper and keep warm.

*4.* Meanwhile poach the eggs. Bring a shallow saucepan of water to a gentle simmer. Crack an egg into a small bowl or ramekin, then slide the egg into the water as close to the water as possible. Using a large spoon, gently fold any stray strands of white around the yolk and cook to your liking. Repeat with the other eggs.

*5.* To serve, place three fritters on each individual plate, place an egg on top and spoon over some of the caramelized onions. Serve immediately.

# Wholewheat Spinach, Pea & Feta Tart

*Wholemeal flour, spinach and peas offer great health benefits for the body and, by marrying them together with an egg mixture, you can experience the taste benefits too!*

| SERVES: | PREP: *35 mins, plus chilling & cooling* | PER SERVING: *439 Kcals* \| *27.1g fat* \| *15.6g sat fat* \| *35.9g carbs* \| *4.9g sugar* |
|---|---|---|
| 6 | COOK: *55 mins–1 hr 15 mins* | *6.2g fibre* \| *16.4g protein* \| *0.7g salt* |

## INGREDIENTS

*15 g/½ oz unsalted butter*
*3 spring onions, thinly sliced*
*200 g/7 oz baby spinach*
*100 g/3½ oz podded peas*
*3 eggs*
*250 ml/9 fl oz milk*
*100 g/3½ oz feta cheese, drained and finely crumbled*
*115 g/4 oz cherry tomatoes*
*sea salt and pepper (optional)*

## PASTRY

*115 g/4 oz unsalted butter, cut into cubes*
*225 g/8 oz wholemeal plain flour, plus 1 tbsp extra to dust*
*2 eggs, beaten*
*salt and pepper (optional)*

1. To make the pastry, put the butter and flour in a mixing bowl and season to taste with salt and pepper, if using. Rub the butter into the flour until it resembles fine breadcrumbs. Gradually mix in enough egg to make a soft but not sticky dough.

2. Lightly dust a work surface with wholemeal flour. Knead the pastry gently, then roll it out on the work surface to a little larger than a 25-cm/10-inch loose-bottomed flan tin. Lift the pastry over the rolling pin, ease it into the tin and press it into the sides. Trim the pastry so that it stands a little above the top of the tin to allow for shrinkage, then prick the base with a fork.

3. Cover the tart case with clingfilm and chill in the refrigerator for 15–30 minutes. Meanwhile, preheat the oven to 190°C/375°F/Gas Mark 5.

4. To make the filling, melt the butter in a frying pan over a medium heat. Add the spring onions and cook for 2–3 minutes, or until softened. Add the spinach, turn the heat to high, and cook, stirring, until wilted. Set aside to cool.

5. Cook the peas in a small saucepan of boiling water for 2 minutes. Drain, then plunge into iced water and drain again. Crack the eggs into a jug, add the milk, season to taste with salt and pepper, if using, and beat with a fork.

6. Line the tart case with a large sheet of baking paper, add baking beans and place on a baking sheet. Bake for 10 minutes, then remove the paper and beans and bake for 5 minutes more, or until the base of the tart is crisp and dry.

7. Drain any cooking juices from the spring onions and spinach into the eggs. Put the onion mixture in the tart case, add the peas, then sprinkle over the cheese. Fork the eggs and milk together once more, then pour into the tart case and dot the tomatoes over the top. Bake for 40–50 minutes, or until set and golden. Leave to cool for 20 minutes, then serve.

# Artichoke & Red Pepper Tortilla

*Traditionally Spanish in origin, this egg-based dish allows you to utilise your culinary flair. Follow the recipe exactly or use it as a guide to create a tortilla delicious by itself or as a side dish.*

| SERVES: | PREP: *25 mins* |
|---|---|
| 8 | COOK: *20–25 mins* |

PER SERVING: *262 Kcals | 21.6g fat | 3.9g sat fat | 5.6g carbs | 2.4g sugar 2.9g fibre | 9.9g protein | 0.9g salt*

## INGREDIENTS

*250 g/9 oz drained artichoke hearts in oil, quartered and 2 tbsp oil reserved*

*175 g/6 oz grilled red peppers in oil, drained and chopped, plus 2 tbsp oil reserved*

*1 large onion, thinly sliced*

*9 large eggs*

*3 tbsp olive oil, for frying*

*salt and pepper (optional)*

1. Heat the reserved oil from the artichokes and peppers in a 25-cm/10-inch frying pan over a high heat. Reduce the heat, add the onion and fry, stirring, for 8–10 minutes, until golden.

2. Beat the eggs in a large bowl. Stir in the artichoke hearts and red peppers and season to taste with salt and pepper, if using.

3. Using a slotted spoon, transfer the onions to the bowl, leaving as much oil in the pan as possible.

4. Add 2–3 tablespoons of olive oil to the pan to make it up to 4 tablespoons. Heat over a high heat, swirling so it coats the side of the pan.

5. Add the egg mixture and smooth the surface. Cook for 30 seconds, then reduce the heat to medium and cook for a further 5–7 minutes, shaking the pan occasionally, until the base is set and using a spatula to loosen the sides of the tortilla.

6. Place a large plate over the top of the pan. Invert the pan and plate together so the tortilla drops on to the plate.

7. Add 1 tablespoon of olive oil to the pan and heat. Slide the tortilla into the pan, cooked-side up. Continue cooking for 3–5 minutes, until the eggs are set and the base is golden brown.

8. Slide the tortilla onto a plate. Cut into wedges and serve hot, warm or at room temperature.

# Ham &
# Egg Pie

*A freshly baked pie is a great source of comfort at the end of a hard day. The ham, egg and onions in this recipe work perfectly alongside each other, great for sharing with family and friends.*

| SERVES: | PREP: *25 mins, plus cooling* | PER SERVING: *603 Kcals │ 33.7g fat │ 18.4g sat fat │ 52.4g carbs │ 2.3g sugar* |
|---|---|---|
| 4 | COOK: *50–55 mins* | *2.6g fibre │ 21.6g protein │ 2.3g salt* |

## INGREDIENTS
*4 eggs*
*175 g/6 oz cooked ham*
*3 spring onions, finely chopped*
*150 ml/5 fl oz milk, plus extra for glazing*
*salt and pepper (optional)*

## PASTRY
*250 g/9 oz plain flour*
*115 g/4 oz butter*
*pinch of salt*
*2 tbsp cold water to mix*

1. Preheat the oven to 200°C/400°F/Gas Mark 6.

2. To make the pastry, put the flour into a bowl, rub in the butter until the mixture resembles fine breadcrumbs, then season with a pinch of salt and add enough water to make a smooth dough.

3. Bring a small saucepan of water to the boil, add two eggs and cook for 8 minutes, then cool quickly in cold water.

4. Divide the pastry in two, one piece slightly larger than the other, and roll out the larger piece to line a 20-cm/8-inch flan tin.

5. Peel and chop the hard-boiled eggs and cut the ham into small pieces. Place the eggs, ham and onions in the pastry case.

6. Beat the remaining eggs with the milk, season to taste with salt and pepper, if using, and pour over the ham mixture.

7. Roll out the other piece of pastry, dampen the edge of the pastry base and lay the lid on top. Seal well and crimp the edges of the pie. Glaze with a little milk and place the pie on a baking sheet.

8. Bake in the preheated oven for 10 minutes then reduce the oven temperature to 180°C/350°F/Gas Mark 4 and bake for a further 30 minutes, until the pastry is golden. Serve warm or cold.

# How To Buy The Best Eggs & Keep Them Fresh

Where you buy your eggs is of course a personal choice, whether it's from a neighbour who keeps a few chickens in their back garden, a farm shop or your local supermarket. Just follow these simple rules to keep your eggs in tip-top condition.

Eggs bought from a shop should always have a 'best before' date stamped on either the egg or the box. Storing eggs in the refrigerator is the safest way, keeping the pointed ends facing downward. If you store them outside the refrigerator, keep them at a constant temperature below 20°C/68°F and make sure that they are stored in date order (you can buy specially designed racks to help with this).

When storing your eggs make sure that they are kept away from strong smelling foods and raw meat. Brown eggshells are less porous than white so brown eggs may keep for longer.

Always wash your hands before and after handling eggs, don't use cracked or dirty eggs and don't re-use leftover egg dishes. The two threads, or chalazae running through the egg white are what secure the yolk to the shell. If you have any spots of blood in the yolk or brown spots in the white simply remove them with a piece of shell, as they are harmless.

The flavour of an egg won't change over time. The flavour difference between a fresh egg and one stored for several weeks in a refrigerator is barely detectable, although the moisture content will change. Because their shells are porous, eggs dehydrate over time.

As the egg gets older, the white becomes more watery and the yolk becomes flatter and less spherical. If you need to check the freshness of a raw egg, simply place it in a bowl of cold water. The older the egg, the larger the pocket of air within it. If the egg drops to the bottom of the bowl on its side, it's very fresh, if it drops more slowly and bounces on the bottom, then it's 2–3 weeks old. An egg that floats on the surface of the water could be several months old and should be discarded.

If you keep your eggs in the refrigerator always remove them about 30 minutes before they are needed. This will help prevent the shells cracking if you are cooking the whole egg in hot water, and the egg white will be firmer.

Eggs will normally keep for around 3 weeks (depending on their freshness when purchased). Once removed from their shells they must be kept covered in the refrigerator. If storing egg yolks on their own, cover with a little cold water to help keep them fresh, but use within 2 days.

Egg whites will keep for up to 2 weeks, or can be frozen for up to 3 months in a sealed container.

Use the freshest eggs you can get for poaching, as they tend to hold their shape best during cooking. Egg whites that are 3–4 days old are better for whisking.

# Fiorentina Pizza

*Bring Italy to your own kitchen with this tempting pizza recipe, served with an egg in the centre for that extra gourmet feel. This recipe makes four 19-cm/7½-inch pizzas.*

| MAKES: | PREP: *40–45 mins, plus rising* | PER PIZZA: *608 Kcals* | *27.1g fat* | *7.5g sat fat* | *61g carbs* | *4.4g sugar* |
|---|---|---|
| 4 PIZZAS | COOK: *13–18 mins* | *4.2g fibre* | *28.1g protein* | *3.3g salt* |

## INGREDIENTS

*300 g/10½ oz strong white bread flour, plus 1 tbsp extra for dusting*
*1 tsp easy-blend dried yeast*
*1½ tsp salt*
*175 ml/6 fl oz hand-hot water*
*1 tbsp olive oil, plus 1 tbsp extra for oiling*

## TOPPING

*250 g/9 oz spinach, washed and drained*
*200 g/7 oz ready-prepared tomato pizza sauce*
*2 garlic cloves, finely chopped*
*25 g/1 oz black olives, stoned and halved*
*2 tbsp garlic olive oil*
*4 eggs*
*85 g/3 oz finely grated Grana Padano cheese*
*salt and pepper (optional)*

1. Sift the flour into a mixing bowl and add the yeast and salt, making a small well in the top. Mix the water and oil together and pour into the bowl, using a round-bladed knife to gradually combine all the flour to make a sticky dough.

2. Lightly flour the work surface and your hands and knead the dough for about 10 minutes, until smooth and elastic.

3. Cover the dough with some lightly oiled clingfilm or a damp tea towel and leave to rise for about an hour, or until it has doubled in size.

4. Knock back the dough by gently kneading for about a minute, then divide into four balls. To roll out the dough, flatten each ball, then, using a rolling pin, roll out on a lightly floured work surface, giving a quarter turn between each roll.

5. Preheat the oven to 220°C/425°F/Gas Mark 7. Place the pizza bases on two baking trays, using a rolling pin to transfer them from the work surface.

6. Wash the spinach and place in a large saucepan with the water clinging to the leaves. Cover and cook for 2–3 minutes until wilted, then squeeze out the excess water between two plates. Return to the pan.

7. Divide the pizza sauce between the four pizza bases, spreading almost to the edges. Scatter over the garlic, top with the spinach and olives and drizzle over the garlic oil.

8. Bake in the preheated oven for 8–10 minutes, then remove from the oven and make a small indentation in the centre of each pizza. Pour an egg into each indentation, scatter over the cheese and season to taste with salt and pepper, if using. Return to the oven and bake for a further 3–5 minutes, or until the eggs are just cooked and the bases are crisp underneath. Serve immediately.

# London Burgers

*Feel free to cook the eggs to your liking, but note that a bit of a runny yolk makes a lovely sauce on these burgers.*

| MAKES: | PREP: *20 mins* | PER BURGER: *551 Kcals* | *30.6g fat* | *13.7g sat fat* | *30.4g carbs* | *6.6g sugar* |
|---|---|---|
| 4 | COOK: *15 mins* | *1.8g fibre* | *35.8g protein* | *1.3g salt* |

## INGREDIENTS

*450 g/1 lb fresh beef mince*
*2 tbsp Worcestershire sauce*
*4 English muffins*
*4 tbsp butter*
*2 tsp vegetable oil*
*4 eggs*
*½ tsp salt*
*½ tsp pepper*

1. Combine the mince with half the Worcestershire sauce in a large bowl. Divide the mixture into four equal-sized portions and shape each portion into a patty about 1 cm/½ inch wider than the muffins, making a dimple in the centre of each patty.

2. Split the muffins and spread each half with butter.

3. Heat a large frying pan over a medium–high heat. Place the muffin halves in the pan buttered side down and cook for about 2 minutes. Put two muffin halves on each of four plates.

4. Add the patties to the pan and cook for about 4 minutes until brown. Turn and cook on the other side for 4 minutes, or until cooked to your liking. Place a burger on one of the muffin halves on each plate and drizzle with the remaining Worcestershire sauce.

5. Add the oil to the pan, swirling to coat. Add the eggs and sprinkle with the salt and pepper. Cover and cook for about 3 minutes until the whites are set and the yolks are beginning to set at the edges.

6. Top each burger with an egg and the top half of a muffin. Serve immediately.

## TRY SOMETHING DIFFERENT

*As well as egg, grilled tomato, bacon, mushrooms, lettuce or green leaves make a tasty filling to these burgers. You could also try serving the egg on top of the bun.*

# Tomato & Caramelized Onion Strata

*This classic American dish combines a mixture of flavours to form a tasty variation on a traditional casserole. Cold or hot, for one or for a group, it's a great way to use up the eggs in your kitchen.*

| SERVES: | PREP: *20 mins* |
|---|---|
| 4 | COOK: *1 hr 5 mins, plus standing* |

PER SERVING: *441 Kcals | 24.8g fat | 10.6g sat fat | 30g carbs | 9.7g sugar 2.4g fibre | 24.7g protein | 1.2g salt*

## INGREDIENTS

*4 tsp olive oil, plus 1 tbsp extra for oiling*
*1 large onion, chopped*
*½ tsp caster sugar*
*1 tbsp snipped fresh chives*
*200 g/7 oz cherry tomatoes*
*125 g/4½ oz day-old French bread, cubed*
*150 g/5½ oz Gruyère cheese, grated*
*3 large eggs*
*350 ml/12 fl oz milk*
*1 tsp Dijon mustard*
*2 tsp chopped fresh thyme*
*pepper (optional)*
*1 tbsp snipped fresh chives, to garnish*
*salad leaves and chutney, to serve (optional)*

1. Preheat the oven to 200°C/400°F/Gas Mark 6. Heat the oil in a frying pan. Add the onion and gently fry for 12–14 minutes until soft and golden brown. Stir in the sugar and cook, stirring, for 1 minute. Remove from the heat and stir in the chives.

2. Meanwhile, place the tomatoes in a lightly oiled roasting tin and roast in the preheated oven for 7–8 minutes until soft and the skins are beginning to split. Reduce the oven temperature to 180°C/350°F/Gas Mark 4.

3. Lightly oil a 1-litre/1¾-pint deep ovenproof dish. Scatter one third of the bread cubes in the base of the dish, followed by a third each of the onions, roast tomatoes and cheese. Season to taste with pepper, if using. Repeat the layers twice more.

4. Place the eggs, milk, mustard and thyme in a jug and whisk together with a fork. Slowly pour the mixture over the bread and vegetables in the dish. Bake for 50 minutes, or until just set in the middle. Leave to stand for 5 minutes, then sprinkle with chives. Serve with salad leaves and chutney, if liked.

## TOP TIP
*The exact cooking time of the strata will depend on the depth of the dish that you've used to cook it in. Once it has set in the middle it is cooked.*

# Egg & Lentil Curry

*Hard-boiled eggs become a great subsidiary to the spiciness of this authentic curry, proving their many capabilities as an incredibly diverse and delicious ingredient once again.*

| SERVES: | PREP: *20–25 mins* |
|---|---|
| 4 | COOK: *45 mins* |

PER SERVING: *349 Kcals* | *21.8g fat* | *6.9g sat fat* | *23.9g carbs* | *5.5g sugar* | *4.1g fibre* | *16.7g protein* | *1.3g salt*

## INGREDIENTS

*3 tbsp ghee or vegetable oil*
*1 large onion, chopped*
*2 garlic cloves, chopped*
*2.5-cm/1-inch piece fresh ginger, chopped*
*½ tsp chilli powder*
*1 tsp ground coriander*
*1 tsp ground cumin*
*1 tsp paprika*
*85 g/3 oz split red lentils*
*475 ml/16 fl oz vegetable stock*
*225 g/8 oz canned chopped tomatoes*
*6 eggs*
*60 ml/2 fl oz coconut milk*
*2 tomatoes, cut into wedges*
*salt (optional)*
*sprigs of fresh coriander, to garnish (optional)*
*chapatis, to serve (optional)*

1. Heat the ghee in a saucepan, add the onion and cook gently for 3 minutes. Stir in the garlic, ginger and spices and cook gently, stirring frequently, for 1 minute.

2. Stir in the lentils, stock and canned tomatoes and bring to the boil. Reduce the heat, cover and simmer, stirring occasionally, for 30 minutes, until the lentils are tender.

3. Meanwhile, place the eggs in a saucepan of cold water and bring to the boil. Reduce the heat and simmer for 10 minutes. Drain and cover immediately with cold water.

4. Stir the coconut milk into the lentil mixture and season to taste with salt, if using. Process the mixture in a blender or food processor until smooth. Return to the pan and heat through.

5. Shell the hard-boiled eggs and cut into quarters. Divide the hard-boiled egg quarters and tomato wedges between warmed serving plates.

6. Spoon over the hot lentil sauce and garnish with sprigs of coriander, if using. Serve hot with chapatis, if liked.

# Skinny Carbonara

*A reduced-fat version of the well-known pasta dish. You can rustle it up in next to no time from ingredients you may already have in the kitchen.*

| SERVES: | PREP: *20 mins* |
|---|---|
| 4 | COOK: *18–20 mins* |

PER SERVING: *523 Kcals | 20g fat | 8.4g sat fat | 57.9g carbs | 3.1g sugar 2.6g fibre | 26g protein | 1.5g salt*

## INGREDIENTS

*300 g/10½ oz dried spaghetti*
*2 large eggs*
*55 g/2 oz freshly grated Parmesan cheese*
*2 tbsp chopped fresh flat-leaf parsley*
*115 g/4 oz pancetta or smoked dry-cure streaky bacon rashers, chopped*
*1 tsp olive oil*
*70 g/2½ oz reduced-fat soft cheese*
*pepper (optional)*

1. Bring a large saucepan of lightly salted water to the boil. Add the spaghetti and cook for 10–12 minutes, or until tender but still firm to the bite.

2. Meanwhile whisk together the eggs, half the Parmesan cheese and the parsley with a fork. Place the pancetta and oil in a large frying pan. Heat gently until the bacon fat starts to run, then fry for 2 minutes, or until lightly browned.

3. Ladle 150 ml/5 fl oz hot cooking water from the spaghetti and reserve, then drain the spaghetti. Add the spaghetti water and soft cheese to the bacon pan, then heat, stirring, until melted and smooth. Remove from the heat.

4. Working quickly, add the hot spaghetti to the bacon pan, pour in the egg mixture and toss everything together – the heat from the pasta and pan will thicken the sauce to a coating consistency. Season to taste with pepper, if using, and divide between warmed bowls. Sprinkle with the remaining cheese and serve immediately.

### TOP TIP
*Try to have everyone sitting at the table ready to eat as this dish is best served straight away; if it stands for a while and starts to look dry, stir in some more hot pasta water or a splash of hot water from the kettle.*

# Meatloaf Stuffed with Quail's Eggs

*The smaller quails eggs are perfect inside this flavoursome meatloaf recipe for a slightly different take on the classic dish.*

| SERVES: | PREP: *40 mins, plus cooling* | PER SERVING: *346 Kcals* │ *24g fat* │ *8.3g sat fat* │ *7g carbs* │ *1.3g sugar* |
|---|---|---|
| 8 | COOK: *1 hr 20 mins, plus resting* | *1.3g fibre* │ *24.9g protein* │ *1.4g salt* |

## INGREDIENTS

*2 tbsp oil, for oiling*
*16 quail's eggs*
*275 g/9¾ oz young leaf spinach*
*½ tsp freshly grated nutmeg, or to taste*
*400 g/14 oz fresh beef mince*
*400 g/14 oz fresh pork mince*
*6 smoked dry-cure streaky bacon rashers,*
 *finely chopped*
*55 g/2 oz fresh white breadcrumbs*
*1 onion, very finely chopped*
*2 garlic cloves, crushed*
*2 tsp fresh thyme leaves*
*2 tsp very finely chopped fresh rosemary*
*salt and pepper (optional)*

1. Lightly oil a 900-g/2-lb loaf tin and line the base with baking paper. Bring a saucepan of water to the boil. Add the eggs and cook over a low heat for 4 minutes to hard boil them. Scoop out with a slotted spoon and place in a bowl of iced water. When completely cool, carefully peel off the shells.

2. Wash the spinach in cold water, drain and place in a large saucepan with the water still clinging to the leaves. Cover and cook for 3–4 minutes until wilted. Drain and refresh under cold running water.

3. Place the spinach between two plates and squeeze out the excess water. Transfer to a bowl. Add the nutmeg and season to taste with salt and pepper, if using.

4. Preheat the oven to 180°C/350°F/Gas Mark 4. Place the beef, pork, bacon, breadcrumbs, onion, garlic, thyme and rosemary in a large bowl. Season to taste with salt and pepper, if using, and mix well.

5. Spread about one third of the mince mixture over the base of the prepared tin, leaving the top uneven. Scatter with half the spinach leaves – you will need to pull them apart – and half the eggs, keeping them away from the sides of the tin.

6. Repeat the layers once more, then cover with the remaining mince mixture. Bake in the preheated oven for 1¼ hours, until the meatloaf has shrunk slightly from the sides of the tin and there are no pink juices running from the centre when tested with a skewer.

7. Pour off the excess juices. Leave the meatloaf to rest for 10 minutes before turning out of the tin. Serve hot or cold.

# Steak Tartare

*Just as tasty raw as they are fried, scrambled or poached, an egg yolk looks tempting on top of this gourmet dish and tastes even better!*

| SERVES: | PREP: *20 mins, plus chilling* |
|---|---|
| 2 | COOK: *n/a* |

PER SERVING: *259 Kcals* | *13g fat* | *4.6g sat fat* | *3.1g carbs* | *1.2g sugar* *0.8g fibre* | *30.9g protein* | *2.2g salt*

## INGREDIENTS

*250 g/9 oz excellent-quality beef fillet or*
*  sirloin steak*
*1 tbsp finely chopped fresh parsley*
*1 tbsp finely chopped capers*
*1 tbsp finely chopped shallots*
*1 tbsp finely chopped gherkins*
*2 dashes hot sauce*
*2 dashes Worcestershire sauce*
*1 tbsp Dijon mustard*
*½ tsp salt*
*2 egg yolks (kept separate)*

1. Chill all the ingredients, a chopping board and mixing bowl for 20 minutes before you begin. Then remove from the refrigerator and very finely chop the steak.

2. Place the steak in the chilled bowl. Add all the remaining ingredients, except the egg yolks, and mix them into the beef with a fork.

3. Shape the mixture into two round patties and make an indent in the middle of each. Place in the refrigerator until ready to serve.

4. To serve, place each patty in the middle of a plate and lay a raw egg yolk in the indent.

## HELPFUL HINT
*Select fine, well-aged steak for this dish and ensure you chop by hand – not mechanically with a mixer – or it will become over-processed and tough.*

# Egg, Meatball & Tomato Tagine

*Put your own twist on this traditional Moroccan stew with meatballs, tomatoes and, of course, eggs to bring something a little different to this timeless dish.*

| SERVES: | PREP: *25–30 mins* | PER SERVING: *564 Kcals* | *42.1g fat* | *15.3g sat fat* | *15g carbs* | *9.2g sugar* |
|---|---|---|
| 4 | COOK: *37–47 mins* | *2.8g fibre* | *30.4g protein* | *1.8g salt* |

## INGREDIENTS

*500 g/1 lb 2 oz lean fresh lamb mince*
  *or fresh beef mince*
*2 tbsp finely chopped fresh parsley*
*1 tsp cumin seeds, crushed*
*1 tsp ground cinnamon*
*½ tsp paprika*
*2 tbsp olive oil*
*salt and pepper (optional)*

## SAUCE

*1 large onion, finely chopped*
*olive oil, for frying (optional)*
*2 garlic cloves, crushed*
*1½ tsp cumin seeds, crushed*
*1 tsp paprika*
*800 g/1 lb 12 oz canned chopped tomatoes*
*½ tsp crushed dried chillies*
*4 eggs*
*salt and pepper (optional)*
*2–3 tbsp chopped fresh coriander, to garnish*

1. To make the meatballs, place the mince, parsley, cumin seeds, cinnamon and paprika in a bowl, season to taste with salt and pepper, if using, and mix well together. Roll into 24 walnut-sized balls.

2. Preheat the oven to 200°C/400°F/Gas Mark 6. Heat the oil in a large frying pan and fry the meatballs for 2–3 minutes, in batches if necessary, until brown all over. Transfer to a plate with a slotted spoon.

3. To make the sauce, add the onion to the pan and fry gently for 10 minutes until soft and golden brown. Add the garlic, cumin seeds and paprika and heat, stirring, for a few seconds, then stir in the tomatoes and chillies. Simmer for 7–10 minutes until the sauce is reduced and very thick. Season to taste with salt and pepper, if using, and remove from the heat.

4. Add the meatballs to the pan. Stir, taking care not to break them up, then transfer to an ovenproof dish. Make four shallow dips in the sauce and carefully break an egg into each one. Bake in the preheated oven for 15–20 minutes until the eggs are just set. Sprinkle with coriander and serve immediately.

### TOP TIP
*You will need to add a little extra oil to the pan in step 3 if the mince you've used was very lean.*

# Desserts

# Baked Passion Fruit Custards

*A tropical treat combining passion fruit pulp with creamy coconut milk and orange flower water to create a delightful dessert.*

| SERVES: | PREP: *20 mins* |
|---|---|
| 4 | COOK: *40–45 mins* |

PER SERVING: *247 Kcals* | *15.4g fat* | *10.2g sat fat* | *19.6g carbs* | *17.1g sugar* | *1.9g fibre* | *9.2g protein* | *0.2g salt*

## INGREDIENTS

*4 passion fruit*
*4 large eggs*
*175 ml/6 fl oz coconut milk*
*55 g/2 oz caster sugar*
*1 tsp orange flower water*

1. Preheat the oven to 180°C/350°F/Gas Mark 4. Halve three passion fruit, scoop out the flesh and rub through a sieve to remove the seeds.

2. Beat together the eggs, passion fruit juice, coconut milk, sugar and orange flower water until smooth.

3. Pour the custard into four 200-ml/7-fl oz ovenproof dishes, place in a baking tin and pour in hot water to reach halfway up the dishes.

4. Bake in the oven for 40–45 minutes or until just set. Scoop the pulp from the remaining passion fruit and spoon a little onto each dish to serve. Serve the custards slightly warm.

### WHY NOT TRY

*These passion fruit custards are equally delicious served chilled. For a dinner party, make a batch in the morning and chill in the refrigerator until required.*

# Chocolate Mousse

*For a luxurious treat, combine chocolate and eggs to create the perfect mousse for a sweet, indulgent fix after dinner.*

| SERVES: | PREP: *20 mins, plus cooling & chilling* | PER SERVING: *392 Kcals* | *26.8g fat* | *14.7g sat fat* | *28.6g carbs* | *20g sugar* |
|---|---|---|
| 6 | COOK: *6–8 mins* | *4.3g fibre* | *7.5g protein* | *0.1g salt* |

## INGREDIENTS

*300 g/10½ oz plain chocolate, broken into small pieces*

*1½ tbsp unsalted butter*

*1 tbsp brandy*

*4 eggs, separated*

*25 g/1 oz finely chopped plain chocolate pieces, to serve*

1. Place the chocolate in a heatproof bowl set over a pan of gently simmering water. Add the butter and melt with the chocolate, stirring, until smooth. Remove from the heat, stir in the brandy and leave to cool slightly. Add the egg yolks and beat until smooth.

2. In a separate bowl, whisk the egg whites until stiff peaks have formed, then fold into the chocolate mixture. Spoon into small serving bowls or pots and level the surfaces. Transfer to the refrigerator and chill for at least 4 hours, or until set.

3. Take the mousse out of the refrigerator and serve immediately, scattered with finely chopped chocolate pieces.

## HELPFUL HINT

*When melting the chocolate, ensure the bottom of the bowl doesn't touch the water, otherwise the chocolate can burn and spoil.*

# Cardamom Waffles with Blackberries & Figs

*Aromatic cardamom adds a wonderful depth of flavour to these fabulous fruit-topped waffles, so dig out your waffle maker and cook up this satisfying weekend family dessert when late-summer blackberries are at their best.*

| SERVES: | PREP: *25 mins, plus resting* | PER SERVING: *422 Kcals* | *17.3g fat* | *7.8g sat fat* | *53.9g carbs* | *23.7g sugar* |
|---|---|---|
| 6 | COOK: *10–17 mins* | *7.3g fibre* | *16.1g protein* | *0.5g salt* |

## INGREDIENTS

*5 large eggs, separated*

*pinch of salt*

*1 tsp ground cardamom*

*50 g/1¾ oz unsalted butter, melted and cooled*

*250 ml/9 fl oz semi-skimmed milk*

*225 g/8 oz wholemeal plain flour*

*1 tbsp olive oil, for brushing*

*150 g/5½ oz Greek-style natural yogurt*

*6 ripe figs, quartered*

*200 g/7 oz blackberries*

*6 tbsp agave syrup, to serve*

1. Place the egg yolks, salt and cardamom into a bowl and beat well with a wooden spoon. Stir in the melted butter. Slowly beat in the milk until fully incorporated. Gradually add the flour until you have a thick batter.

2. In a separate bowl, whisk the egg whites until they form stiff peaks and gently fold them into the batter. Leave the batter to rest for at least an hour, but preferably overnight.

3. Heat the waffle maker according to the manufacturers' instructions. Brush with a little oil and spoon the batter onto the waffle iron. Cook for 4–5 minutes, or until golden. Keep each waffle warm, under foil, in a low oven until you are ready to serve.

4. Serve each waffle immediately, topped with yogurt, fig quarters, blackberries and agave syrup.

### WHY NOT TRY

*Vary the fruit you use to add different flavours and different levels of sweetness, whilst also providing a healthier edge to the dessert.*

# Crème Caramel

Sweet, smooth and ideal as a light dessert, the eggs aid the characteristic silkiness of a crème caramel.

| SERVES: | PREP: *25 mins, plus cooling & chilling* | PER SERVING: *377 Kcals | 12.7g fat | 6.1g sat fat | 57.5g carbs | 56.7g sugar* |
|---|---|---|
| 4 | COOK: *1 hr 10 mins–1 hr 25 mins* | *0.3g fibre | 9.7g protein | 0.3g salt* |

## INGREDIENTS

*1 tbsp butter, for greasing*

*200 g/7 oz caster sugar*

*4 tbsp water*

*½ lemon*

*500 ml/17 fl oz milk*

*1 vanilla pod*

*2 large eggs*

*2 large egg yolks*

1. Preheat the oven to 160°C/325°F/Gas Mark 3. Lightly grease the base and sides of four ramekin dishes. To make the caramel, place 75 g/2¾ oz sugar with the water in a saucepan over a medium–high heat and cook, stirring, until the sugar dissolves. Boil until the syrup turns a deep golden brown. Immediately remove from the heat and squeeze in a few drops of lemon juice. Divide evenly between the ramekin dishes.

2. Pour the milk into a saucepan. Slit the vanilla pod lengthways and, using the tip of a knife, scrape out the seeds into the milk. Drop the vanilla pod in as well. Bring to the boil, remove the saucepan from the heat and stir in the remaining sugar, stirring until it dissolves. Reserve.

3. Beat the eggs and yolks together in a bowl and pour the milk mixture over them, whisking. Remove the vanilla pod. Strain the mixture into a bowl and divide evenly between the ramekins.

4. Place the dishes in a roasting tin. Boil a kettle and carefully pour the hot water into the tin so that it comes two-thirds of the way up the sides of the dishes.

5. Bake in the preheated oven for 1–1¼ hours, or until a knife inserted in the centre comes out clean. Leave to cool completely. Cover with clingfilm and leave to chill in the refrigerator for at least 24 hours.

6. Run a round-bladed knife around the edge of each dish. Place an up-turned serving plate, with a rim, on top of each dish, then invert the plate and dish, giving a sharp shake halfway over. Lift off the ramekin dishes and serve immediately.

# Apricot & Rosemary Clafoutis

*This baked French dessert is a comforting, sweet treat, easy to prepare and ideal straight from the oven.*

| SERVES: | PREP: *20–25 mins* |
|---|---|
| 6 | COOK: *25 mins* |

PER SERVING: *469 Kcals* | *26.8g fat* | *15.2g sat fat* | *48.5g carbs* | *35.9g sugar* *1.4g fibre* | *9.2g protein* | *0.2g salt*

## INGREDIENTS
*1 tbsp butter*
*2 tbsp caster sugar, for dusting*
*300 g/10½ oz apricots, halved*
  *and stoned*
*6 eggs, beaten*
*250 ml/9 fl oz double cream*
*150 g/5½ oz caster sugar*
*1 tsp finely chopped fresh rosemary*
*90 g/3¼ oz plain flour, sifted*

1.  Preheat the oven to 200°C/400°F/Gas Mark 6. Grease a large, oval gratin dish, about 26 cm/10½ inches in diameter with the butter and dust with 1 tablespoon of sugar.

2.  Spread the apricots evenly cut-side up over the base of the prepared dish and set aside.

3.  In a large bowl, whisk the eggs, cream and sugar together with the rosemary until light and fluffy, then fold in the flour. Pour the mixture carefully over the apricots, taking care not to dislodge them.

4.  Bake in the preheated oven for 25 minutes, or until puffed up and set. Dust with the remaining sugar and serve warm or at room temperature.

### TOP TIP
*Put the gratin dish with the apricots on a baking tray before you add the batter mixture. That way it is easier to transfer to the oven without spilling the batter or upsetting the layout of the fruit.*

# Essential Equipment

There are many different gadgets available to help with cooking eggs. Your choice of these will depend on your budget, how you like to use and cook with eggs and how much storage space you have in your kitchen.

## EGG SEPARATORS

These simple devices come in various guises. They separate the yolks from the whites and prevent the shell breaking into the egg. These are really useful if you like making meringues.

## EGG CODDLER

Coddled eggs are gently steamed eggs cooked in specially designed ceramic pots with lids that seal tightly to keep out moisture. The coddlers are lightly buttered before the eggs are added with a little cream and seasoning. The coddlers are then placed in a saucepan of boiling water and simmered for 4 minutes. The pan is removed from the heat and the coddlers are left to stand for about 6 minutes. You could substitute ramekin dishes and cover them with foil, but egg coddlers are very neat and tidy.

## POACHING DEVICES

Of course you can poach eggs without any gadgets, just by adding an egg to a saucepan of boiling water, but if you want guaranteed perfection, then try one of the many devices available to help with the task. These take two main forms: either a shallow pan with four removable pods to hold the eggs, or individual silicone egg poaching pods that can be added to a saucepan of boiling water. You can also poach eggs in the microwave, using specially designed lidded containers.

## TIMING DEVICES

Again, there are lots to choose from. Whether it's a traditional timer with sand or a colour-changing egg-shaped timer to go in the saucepan, which will tell you when your egg is cooked, the choice is yours.

## EGG PRICKER

This little device is essentially a stand with a small pin at the base onto which the egg is gently pressed. The hole is small enough that the egg won't run out but means that the shell shouldn't break during cooking.

## EGG COOKER

An electric timed gadget that cooks the eggs by steaming them in their shells until soft- or hard-boiled, or poaching them to perfection in a mould.

## SILICONE/METAL EGG COOKING RINGS

These simply hold the eggs in shape while they fry in the pan, for those of you who love all things perfect! Otherwise, if you usually fry only 1 egg, you could invest in an individual egg pan.

## BOILED EGG TOPPER

If you struggle with cutting the tops from hot, freshly boiled eggs, then these are a great idea. They come in a variety of types, and take the top cleanly off the egg without any rogue pieces of shell getting into your soft-boiled egg.

## EGG SPOON

If you're a real lover of soft-boiled eggs, then this is for you. Designed specifically for eating boiled eggs, it has a shorter handle, slightly more pointed tip and a deeper bowl than a teaspoon, making it easier to get into the egg.

# CRÈME BRÛLÉE

*This dessert has long been a favourite of many people because the ingredients work in perfect harmony to produce a mouth-watering dish.*

| SERVES: | PREP: *25 mins, plus cooling* |
|---------|------------------------------|
| 6 | COOK: *45–60 mins* |

PER SERVING: *510 Kcals* | *44.1g fat* | *26.3g sat fat* | *24.6g carbs* | *23.9g sugar*
*trace fibre* | *4.1g protein* | *trace salt*

## INGREDIENTS

*500 ml/17fl oz double cream*
*1 vanilla pod*
*100 g/3½ oz caster sugar, plus extra 2 tbsp*
 *for the topping*
*6 egg yolks*

1. Preheat the oven to 160°C/325°F/Gas Mark 3.

2. Pour the cream into a small saucepan. Split the vanilla pod in half lengthways. Scrape the seeds into the pan, then chop the pod into little pieces and add that too. Heat the cream to boiling, then reduce the heat and simmer gently for 5 minutes.

3. Put the sugar and egg yolks in a heatproof bowl and beat with a spoon until well mixed. Pour the hot cream into the egg mixture, beating (not whisking) as you pour, until it's nicely thickened. Pass this custard through a fine sieve into another bowl or jug. Pour the mixture into a wide, flat dish and lay this in a roasting tray. Boil a kettle and carefully pour the hot water into the tray so that it comes halfway up the sides of the crème brûlée dish.

4. Place in the preheated oven and bake for about 30–45 minutes, or until the custard has just set.

5. Remove from the oven and leave to cool to room temperature. Sprinkle some caster sugar over the custard and then gently caramelize it using a kitchen blow torch, or under a very hot grill. Leave to cool for a few minutes then serve.

# Classic Meringues

*Light and fluffy like clouds, these meringues are topped with a sweet, creamy topping and fresh strawberries.*

| MAKES: | PREP: *35 mins, plus cooling* |
|---|---|
| 10 | COOK: *1 hr 10 mins* |

PER TOPPED MERINGUE: *289 Kcals | 14.4g fat | 8.9g sat fat | 38.5g carbs 36.5g sugar | 1g fibre | 2.3g protein | trace salt*

## INGREDIENTS

*4 egg whites*

*300 g/10½ oz caster sugar*

*2 tsp white wine vinegar*

*2 tsp cornflour*

*300 ml/10 fl oz double cream*

*4 tbsp icing sugar*

*1 tsp vanilla extract*

*500 g/1 lb 2 oz strawberries, hulled and halved if large*

1. Preheat the oven to 180°C/350°F/Gas Mark 4. Place a round cutter on top of a sheet of baking paper and carefully trace round it with a pencil. Draw five circles on one sheet and repeat on another sheet. Put the baking paper, drawn-side down, on two baking sheets.

2. Put the egg whites in a large bowl, then whisk using an electric hand mixer until the egg whites stand in firm, stiff peaks.

3. Whisk in the caster sugar a tablespoonful at a time until the mixture is shiny and stiff, then whisk in the vinegar and cornflour.

4. Spoon the mixture onto the circles on the baking paper and make a dip in the centre of each with the back of the spoon.

5. Bake for 10 minutes, then turn the oven down to 120°C/250°F/Gas Mark ½ and cook for 1 hour. Remove from the oven and leave the meringues to cool a little, then move to a wire rack.

6. Whisk together the cream, icing sugar and vanilla extract in another large bowl until the mixture stands in soft peaks. Spoon the cream into the dips in the meringues and top with strawberries.

# Tiramisù

*This classic Italian dessert is always a winner. This version is made with mascarpone cheese, but for a healthier version you could use low-fat cream cheese.*

| SERVES: | PREP: *25–30 mins, plus chilling* |
|---|---|
| 6 | COOK: *5 mins* |

PER SERVING: *619 Kcals | 40.4g fat | 27.5g sat fat | 43.8g carbs | 34.1g sugar 1.3g fibre | 8.3g protein | 0.2g salt*

## INGREDIENTS

*4 egg yolks*
*100 g/3½ oz caster sugar*
*1 tsp vanilla extract*
*500 g/1 lb 2 oz mascarpone cheese*
*2 egg whites*
*175 ml/6 fl oz strong black coffee*
*125 ml/4 fl oz rum or brandy*
*24 sponge fingers*
*2 tbsp cocoa powder*
*2 tbsp finely grated plain chocolate*

1. Whisk the egg yolks with the sugar and vanilla extract in a heatproof bowl set over a saucepan of barely simmering water.

2. When the mixture is pale and the whisk leaves a ribbon trail when lifted, remove the bowl from the heat and set aside to cool. Whisk occasionally to prevent a skin from forming.

3. When the egg yolk mixture is cool, whisk in the mascarpone until thoroughly combined.

4. Whisk the egg whites in a separate clean bowl until they form soft peaks, then gently fold them into the mascarpone mixture.

5. Combine the coffee and rum in a shallow dish. Briefly dip eight of the sponge fingers in the mixture, then arrange in the base of a deep, wide serving dish.

6. Spoon one third of the mascarpone mixture on top, spreading it out evenly. Repeat the layers twice, finishing with the mascarpone mixture. Chill in the refrigerator for at least 1 hour.

7. Sift the cocoa evenly over the top and sprinkle with the chocolate. Serve immediately.

# Baked Lemon Cheesecake

*Eggs are vital in making this cheesecake as smooth and creamy as it can be, whilst the lemons provide a tangy edge to balance the sweetness.*

| SERVES: | PREP: *25 mins, plus chilling* |
|---|---|
| 8 | COOK: *45 mins* |

PER SERVING: *353 Kcals | 24.1g fat | 11.9g sat fat | 31.2g carbs | 20.6g sugar*
*1.2g fibre | 11.5g protein | 0.4g salt*

## INGREDIENTS

*55 g/2 oz butter, plus 1 tbsp extra for greasing*
*175 g/6 oz gingernut biscuits, crushed*
*3 lemons*
*300 g/10½ oz ricotta cheese*
*200 g/7 oz Greek-style yogurt*
*4 eggs*
*1 tbsp cornflour*
*100 g/3½ oz caster sugar*
*strips of lemon zest, to decorate (optional)*

1. Preheat the oven to 180°C/350°F/Gas Mark 4. Grease a 20-cm/8-inch round springform cake tin and line with baking paper.

2. Melt the butter and stir in the biscuit crumbs. Press into the base of the prepared cake tin. Chill in the refrigerator until firm.

3. Meanwhile, finely grate the rind and squeeze the juice from the lemons and put into a large bowl. Add the ricotta, yogurt, eggs, cornflour and caster sugar, and whisk until a smooth batter is formed.

4. Carefully spoon the mixture into the tin. Bake in the preheated oven for 40–45 minutes, or until just firm and golden brown.

5. Cool the cheesecake completely in the tin, then run a knife around the edge to loosen and turn out onto a serving plate. Decorate with strips of lemon zest, if using, and serve.

# Lemon Angel Food Cake

*Some say this light and airy sponge cake originated in India. But many Southern Americans believe that a frugal ancestor created the cake in order to avoid discarding egg whites left over from other recipes.*

| SERVES: | PREP: *25–30 mins, plus cooling* |
|---|---|
| 10 | COOK: *35–45 mins* |

PER SERVING: *168 Kcals | 0.6g fat | trace sat fat | 35.3g carbs | 25.3g sugar 0.2g fibre | 5.3g protein | 0.3g salt*

## INGREDIENTS

*12 egg whites*
*1¼ tsp cream of tartar*
*pinch of salt*
*200–300 g/7–10½ oz caster sugar*
*125 g/4½ oz soft cake flour, sifted*
*1 tsp lemon extract*
*½ tsp vanilla extract*

1. Preheat the oven to 180°C/350°F/Gas Mark 4. Beat the egg whites with a hand-held electric mixer on high speed until light and foamy. Add the cream of tartar and salt and beat again until they hold soft peaks.

2. Add the sugar, 2 tablespoons at a time, beating until the mixture holds stiff peaks. Sprinkle the flour into the mixture, a little at a time, folding in each addition carefully. Fold in the lemon extract and vanilla extract.

3. Pour the batter into an ungreased 25-cm/10-inch ring tin, spreading evenly. Bake in the preheated oven for 35–45 minutes, or until the cake springs back when lightly touched.

4. Remove the cake from the oven and immediately invert the tin onto a wire rack. Leave to cool for at least 1 hour, then remove the cake from the tin and serve.

## WHY NOT TRY

*Use 1 teaspoon of fresh lemon juice instead of lemon extract. For an extra lemony twist, also add 1½ teaspoons of freshly grated lemon zest, along with the juice.*

# Goan Layered Coconut Cake

*This traditional Goan dessert is best served warm with ice cream and it can be preserved for a long time, so nothing goes to waste!*

| SERVES: | PREP: *35 mins, plus chilling* | PER SERVING: *406 Kcals* \| *22.5g fat* \| *15.1g sat fat* \| *47.2g carbs* \| *31.1g sugar* |
|---|---|---|
| 10 | COOK: *1 hr 50 mins–2 hrs 15 mins* | *0.6g fibre* \| *5.7g protein* \| *0.2g salt* |

## INGREDIENTS

*400 ml/14 fl oz coconut milk*

*300 g/10½ oz golden caster sugar*

*10 egg yolks, lightly beaten*

*200 g/7 oz plain flour*

*½ tsp freshly grated nutmeg*

*¼ tsp freshly ground cardamom seeds*

*pinch of ground cloves*

*¼ tsp ground cinnamon*

*100 g/3½ oz butter, plus extra*

*1 tbsp for greasing*

1. Preheat the oven to 200°C/400°F/Gas Mark 6. Lightly grease a 17-cm/6½-inch non-stick, round cake tin and line with baking paper.

2. Pour the coconut milk into a saucepan and stir in the sugar. Heat gently for 8–10 minutes, stirring until the sugar has dissolved. Remove from the heat and gradually add the beaten egg yolks, whisking all the time so that the eggs do not scramble and the mixture is smooth. Sift in the flour and spices and stir to make a smooth batter.

3. Melt the butter, then add a tablespoon to the prepared tin and spread over the base. Pour an eighth of the batter into the tin and spread to coat the base evenly. Bake in the preheated oven for 10–12 minutes, or until set.

4. Remove from the oven and brush another spoonful of the melted butter over the top, followed by another eighth of the batter. Return to the oven and cook for 10–12 minutes, or until set.

5. Repeat this process until all the butter and batter has been used up, baking for a further 20–25 minutes, or until the top is golden brown and the cake is firmly set. Remove from the oven and allow to cool in the tin.

6. When cool, remove from the tin, cover with clingfilm and chill in the refrigerator for 4–6 hours before serving.

# Raspberry & Mascarpone Ice Cream

*Fresh raspberries and extra creaminess from the mascarpone mean you will be fighting people off the last scoops of this classic ice cream.*

| SERVES: | PREP: *25 mins, plus freezing* |
|---------|-------------------------------|
| 8 | COOK: *5–10 mins* |

PER SERVING: *285 Kcals | 28.6g fat | 16.5g sat fat | 3.9g carbs | 1.2g sugar 0.8g fibre | 4.2g protein | 0.1g salt*

## INGREDIENTS

*1 large egg, plus 4 large egg yolks*
*2½ tbsp stevia (sugar substitute)*
*100 g/3½oz mascarpone cheese*
*1 tsp vanilla extract*
*400 ml/14 fl oz double cream*
*80 g/2¾ oz raspberries, halved*

1. Crack the egg into a large heatproof bowl, add the yolks and stevia, and whisk with an electric hand-held mixer for 30 seconds. Place over a saucepan of gently simmering water, making sure the bowl doesn't touch the water, and whisk until the mixture is pale and airy. This cooks the eggs and makes a sweet custard, but be careful not to overcook them.

2. Pour cold water into a basin and put the custard bowl into it, so the base of the bowl is in the water, to cool. Continue to whisk for 2 minutes, then lift the bowl out of the water and set aside.

3. Put the mascarpone and vanilla in another large bowl and whisk briefly until loose. Pour in the cream and whisk again until it forms soft peaks.

4. Using a metal spoon, gently fold the custard into the cream mixture, preserving as much air as possible. Stir in the raspberries.

5. Pour the mixture into a freezerproof container, cover with a lid and freeze for 4 hours, or until set. Take the ice cream out of the freezer 10 minutes before you serve it to allow it to soften. Scoop it into glasses or small bowls and serve immediately.

### HELPFUL HINT

*To make it even easier to scoop out the ice cream, put your ice-cream scoop in a jug of hot water for a couple of minutes before using it.*

# Index